WOMEN
AT FIFTY

WOMEN
AT FIFTY

MICHÈLE THIRIET
& SUZANNE KEPES, M.D.

Translated by Linda Butler Koseoglu

•

SCHOCKEN BOOKS / NEW YORK

First published by Schocken Books 1987
10 9 8 7 6 5 4 3 2 1   87 88 89 90

English translation copyright © 1987 by Schocken Books Inc.

Library of Congress Cataloging-in-Publication Data
Thiriet, Michèle.
Women at fifty.
Translation of: Femmes à 50 ans.
Bibliography: p.
Includes index.
1. Middle aged women.   I. Népès, Suzanne.   II. Title.
HQ1059.4.T4713   1987   305.4   87–9617

Design by Cassandra J. Pappas
Manufactured in the United States of America
ISBN 0–8052–4033–0

Contents

WOMEN
AT FIFTY

Introduction

TIME PASSES. It passes with work, with pleasure, births, sorrows, leisure. With years. And then one day we hit fifty, and time stops short.

For women, fifty is more than a birthday. It is a threshold, a coming face to face with aging and a harsh reality: menopause. A foretaste of retirement, before its time.

Menopause. The word is spoken only among women. It carries with it an aura of wrinkles and slack flesh, hysteria, forced sterility, going to seed. It is a matter of "female problems" and nerves—the butt of jokes.

Such was the situation for most of our mothers and grandmothers. Is it still, at least a little? How do we women of today live with it? Within the space of a few weeks, an ill-defined discomfort and strange sensations set in insidiously—unaccustomed new effects that throw us off balance, threatening our way of inhabiting our body and relying on it. We run to the mirror but find nothing special that we do not already know, if it isn't that time is settling in around our waist and on our features, silently leaving its traces from day to day.

So we are crossing the line; we are now among those women we have heard referred to in pitying or sarcastic tones as being "of an unfortunate age." Is it now my turn to become a caricature of a woman, precariously and uncomfortably poised between youth and old age, waiting to retire discreetly from the scene? Could this really be happening to me?

It is unacceptable, somehow, to speak of decline while we are still full of life, especially since the road from a vigorous prime to decrepitude is a long one. But the indications are there, confirmed by laboratory results. Is my body escaping my control? What can I do about this troubling change?

Some deny it. "I don't notice anything." "Menopause, what's that?" Others give in. "Let nature have its way. Suffering from being female is part of our lot."

Still others—and we are among these—reject these alternatives, knowing that rejection is possible, that others struggle and rebel. What is important for us is to see clearly, to take stock, to know where and how to go forward and what to take along on this journey toward new horizons.

Such concerns are at the core of this book, which grew out of a meeting between the two women who ultimately decided to write it. What began as a simple medical checkup—one of us pushed by the reality of years to consult the other, who by virtue of her profession and greater age was in a position to respond—soon took on wider implications. It was as if the encounter were freighted with the case histories of hundreds and hundreds of women seen in the consulting rooms and working groups over long years of our respective professional lives as gynecologist and social worker. The doctor was dedicated to the fight against the injustices of illness, the injustices committed against those whose bodies fail them or change. And both were revolted to see so many women, full of life and in good health, put aside, shelved as useless, with the consequent loss of all self-confidence.

It is heartwrenching to see their difficulties, their powerlessness—because no one helps them. Yet the source of their vitality has in no way dried up. Their role is still necessary, their experience still precious. We reject in the strongest terms the discredit cast on this period of a woman's life, the mournful and shame-ridden resignation we too frequently encounter among them.

It is legitimate to ask why our Western culture is so quick to waste what took so much time and painstaking effort to build: an adult woman. Could it be because menopause speaks to us indirectly of old age and death? In a culture increasingly obsessed with the fear of death (even while modern medicine is pushing it further and further away), everything conspires to ignore the warning sounded by a woman's body at fifty: the reminder of life's finitude.

In order to flee this unbearable idea, fashion as well as the gaze of men focuses on the idealized image of the eternally young and beautiful—and hence desirable—woman, giving rise to a gigantic public and private cult. The threat this entails for women, acutely aware of the growing distance between themselves and the ideal model, is obvious. From there, it is but a short step to that sense of guilt so familiar to women, that anxiety of not being what is needed, where and when it is needed—the anxiety of not being able to do or be what is expected of them.

Despite this reminder of age and, beyond, of death, women know that they have another twenty-five years ahead of them. They do not want to waste these years or live as marginals, saddled with a thousand discomforts they are called upon to hide as much as possible.

But there are other ways of writing this next chapter life offers. It can be filled with other pleasures, other enthusiasms, new and stimulating opportunities. Far from having to feel useless or washed up, women can heed other voices. They can act.

In writing these lines, we are aware that some women are not able to rise to the challenge. We know that women do not all have the same opportunities and that social inequities become cruelly evident at this juncture, just as they do later with retirement. The elegant silhouettes of the privileged have little in common with the worn bodies, depleted by work or numerous childbirths, of their less fortunate sisters. Some are at the height of stimulating careers; others are doomed to repeat the same gestures that stultify their talents and desires. Has there ever been a political platform that truly denounced this injustice?

But whatever our station, whether we are rich or poor, famous or ordinary, sooner or later we are all affected by the sarcasm or indirect rejection of a public opinion united in its negativism concerning the woman's "change of life." It is as if we were placed in front of one of those fun-house mirrors that reflect back a grotesque distortion. Then come the diffuse fears, sadness, and uncertainty about the future.

That, too, revolted us, and through this book we wanted to refuse to be the plaything tossed away when no longer wanted, used up like some consumer item. We want to encourage women to keep their grip on life, because we are convinced—and witnesses to the fact—that some can succeed.

We know that if our vital energy is not stifled, deflected, or otherwise interfered with, we can enjoy good health, strength, and the capital of experience for several decades to come. Difficulties and hardships can bring in their wake surprising opportunities and welcome changes. Youth has no edge on us in handling life's situations effectively. Age gives another kind of courage and other resources.

Why not seize the opportunity offered by this new stage in life to break free of routines? Aging can be a springboard just as easily as an obstacle. We are not old in the sense our grandmothers were with the same number of years—certainly not at fifty. Let's take advantage of it.

Not that we have any illusions. Our intention in this book is not to deceive anyone about the reality of aging or to downplay the accelerating effect menopause can have on that process. We cannot deny that it has unpleasant repercussions on our physical state, not to mention our morale. These symptoms can appear in the strongest women, those least likely to "let themselves go." Yet we are constantly assaulted, in print and by hearsay, with old wives' tales affirming that "hot flashes" are limited to softies and hysterics. It isn't true, and in any case, what exactly is meant by these contemptuous terms?

Be that as it may, today there are ways to help all women. If we are approaching fifty or have reached it, let us begin by taking a sober, responsible look at the actual functioning of our bodies, our tools for living. In order to give the body the kind of maintenance best suited to the changes wrought by menopause, we have first to evaluate its condition after all these years of use, not to say disuse. Too many of us are ignorant or fearful of the medical field and its progress. At the other extreme, there are those who haphazardly latch on to whatever formula comes along from whatever source, medical or otherwise.

We need the help of a competent and understanding doctor, but this does not take any of the burden off us. He or she needs our full cooperation, especially in providing feedback concerning our individual receptiveness to the prescriptions offered. Our success in getting through this period will depend on our conviction, our energy, and our choice of the treatment to be undertaken.

Menopause is not the first hormonal revolution we have been through as women. Puberty in its time modified our organism, installing in us a new order. The first pregnancy, too, was an important innovation, with its internal transformations, its joys and depressions. Even more familiar to us are the discontinuous rhythm of our menstrual cycle and its hormonal variations, which we generally know how to take in our stride. We are accustomed, therefore, to undergoing constant and secret transformations. This facility for adaptation has ripened in us, and today it is an asset that can give us the confidence we need to tackle the new adventure that lies ahead.

· PART 1 ·

Where We Are Now

· CHAPTER 1 ·

Taking Stock

WE ARE the generation who spent our early youth or adolescence during the war. We are no longer wide-eyed, no longer facing our first hardships in life. But even though many of us are in the same situation, each must embark upon this new page in our history as an individual, and too often alone. It is not easy to be a woman and to have reached the outer limits of fifty.

Nor is it acceptable to turn it into melodrama. And yet . . .

Behind us lie the "tender years," the awkward age of adolescence. That seems like only yesterday. Adulthood—we've scarcely started in on that! Middle age—could that be me? Change of life—already? Why not "getting on in years," "over the hill," or even "gone to seed," like merchandise no longer fit for consumption? Expressions such as "old age" and "despite her advanced years" loom up suffocatingly. "Let me breathe and live! I am barely fifty! These five decades, this half-century, sped by so quickly, more quickly with each passing year!"

Some wake up to the realization that their youth has slipped by without their really having enjoyed it; they only recognize it once it has gone, and feel cheated. For those who were able to enjoy it, there is regret, the wish they could linger longer.

Swindled, fulfilled, frustrated, resigned—we run the whole gamut of feelings as we reach this pivotal point. And here we all are, as if perched on or clinging to a steep rooftop, a little out of breath, hoping we will not have to climb down again too quickly or fall on our face.

From up here, if we are not overcome by dizziness, we can survey the terrain. Perched more or less comfortably on our pinnacle, we can rest for a while and examine all the horizons, even the most distant. We can see where we have come from, where we are now, and which roads are to be taken or avoided when we set off again tomorrow. To understand the subtle cloud of disgrace that hangs over the age of fifty—for women far more than for men—we must first explore the landscape of the past. Was it always like that?

Our historical place as women living in the second half of the twentieth century is not at first glance comparable to that of our ancestors, even our relatively recent ones, a large number of whom died in childbirth or long before they reached our age. And childbirth was not the only risk; malnutrition and epidemics rendered powerless both physicians and princes. The women who managed to survive earned the respect often accorded to those who, having escaped great perils, are believed to have retained some magic power from their brush with the hereafter. Rich in their experience of danger, these matrons knew how to go about assisting at births and deaths. The community depended on their knowledge and wisdom, and feared their authority—an authority that, at the time, always came from above. The age of these women gave it to them. To escape their power when they were no longer needed, men and women used ridicule against them. Those who were particularly troublesome were branded as witches.

What remains in us of these distant grandmothers? What images of them still linger in our unconscious?

Closer to our own time, at the end of the nineteenth century, those of our sex were practically old women by the time they reached thirty, required by the laws of propriety to settle into somber and modest garments and to assume the gestures and bearing appropriate to the withered but admirable old maids or matrons they were expected to be. The profound social differences of the time counted for nothing—peasants, workers, and ladies all donned the same mask and shared the same fate: fleeting youth, precarious and brief maturity, and, for the lucky ones, a doubtless morose old age.

During those same years, an event of capital significance occurred: the importance of hygiene during childbirth was discovered. A Viennese physician observed a significant drop in the mortality rate among new mothers whose midwives had had the insight to wash their hands before delivery. This simple measure, the result of pure intuition, saved countless lives thereafter. Life expectancy has increased greatly since then, thanks to yet other new strides in medicine and hygiene. We can now expect, on the average, to live another twenty-five years beyond our fiftieth.

If we divide our lives roughly into successive stages, we will note that we spend about twelve years being formed by our childhood and six to eight years entering and going through puberty. Then we have some twenty years at the height of our productive powers. Indeed, it has become increasingly easy to "program" one's childbearing, making it possible to "get it over with" and move on to other tasks, other forms of productivity and creativity.

Adding it all up, and taking into account an average life expectancy of seventy-five years, we see that the chapter now opening will undoubtedly be the longest in our existence. That would be cause for rejoicing if the phrase "quantity does not necessarily mean quality" were not ringing in our ears. Fear of the unknown and fear of the void loom up to cloud our view of the future, especially because we have to contend with preconceived notions deeply rooted in our unconscious: pathetic images of menopausal women dredged up from a bygone era, with no relevance to today, but resonating in us like a threat.

Realistically, we know that even while our life expectancy is growing, the means of keeping active and healthy are better known than ever before and should be within reach of a growing number of women. More and more of us are not old at our age and don't feel so, either physically or mentally, despite the traces the years have left with greater or lesser emphasis on all of us.

Are we not pioneers of sorts, seeking new ways for women to live these years? As such, we are still misunderstood. And if our contemporaries have not yet been able to adjust to this new reality and still cling to their old prejudices, it is up to us to be convincing examples of the positive change in women our age.

What we experience every day tells us that, far from being "out of it," we are at the very heart of things. While many of us do not hold prestigious or powerful positions, we often have a number of concurrent obligations—economic, emotional, moral. And all this responsibility must be assumed under social conditions that are at once sheltered and increasingly difficult.

We have scarcely had time to think of ourselves and our own needs: career changes, what to do after the childrearing years, the possibility of entering the workforce or becoming active in the community, early retirement plans for our spouse, or, farther down the road, for ourselves. And all the while we are otherwise occupied, our body is following its own logic, which we do not understand. It goes off on a tangent for an unknown destination— a turncoat in the heat of battle! In being far from ourselves and our needs, we are at the very core of the feminine condition.

Leafing through dozens of books about women as well as feminist tracts of varying degrees of militancy—writings not so much on women as on Woman—we are struck by the unspoken assumption that we are a compact and fully formed entity, absolutely unchanging, whether we are seven or seventy-seven. The only exception appears to be in the old saws about women's inconstancy that men like to invoke. But deep down, they too dream of us as unutterably changeless. They speak of woman as if she were an unchanging river which, beginning small, flows steadily until it loses itself in the sands. Or as if time's marks on her were invisible and regular. As if she were an immobile statue of flesh, languishing on her pedestal in public gardens, fixing eyes of stone on children playing, out of time. If we changed, and if the change were recognized, we would disturb the order of dreams.

What will become of the "eternal woman," eternally the same, always pliable, always ready to fulfill without complaint her tasks of seduction, production, and reproduction? Well, we never were made of marble. Our reality is otherwise, and it can be of particular use to us today. Our entire life as a woman is there, to remind us.

Women feel within themselves permanent, continuous change rather than linear movement, and that is our paradox. The rhythm and variations of our body lead us constantly to adapt to what the body secretes, produces, or ceases to produce. We feel ourselves like the phases of the moon, the tides, the seasons, like the earth which changes faces and fertility even while none of these transformations compromise the coming of the next harvest.

In all this lies our difference. It is up to us to look at ourselves and recognize our originality—and to make use of it.

The fifty-year mark, menopause: these are changes that have long been in the making. The groundwork was laid by all the successive little stages that constitute our ebb and flow each month, this movement of life that rises and falls, warms and cools us, and choreographs in us a veritable ballet of hormones. Being women, we are naturally suited for transitions, so it is not nature alone that stands in the way of a smooth journey. We know that not all women experience this period as a calamity. It is perfectly possible to go through this intermediary stage without much difficulty and to discover at the other end the novelty of a more stable life. But we cannot consider this problem as if it were resolved for everyone—to do so would serve as a kind of reproach to those women who suffer profoundly from the change of life. Their lives speak too strongly, and with too much truth, for us to silence them. And even if to lesser degrees, we can all recognize ourselves in their stories.

Monique. 51 years old. No children, although she raised her husband's. Her menopause began when she was 46; she was 51 when she came in for a consultation. She complained of painful intercourse and had heard that it is not uncommon at her age. She had already seen a doctor but had not dared tell him the true reason for her visit: "There are some things you just can't say to a man . . ." She felt the same reticence with her husband. The couple lived in a state of crisis. He was attracted to young women and had affairs. By way of explanation, he would sing snatches of popular songs: "Some day I'll leave, I won't finish my days with an old bag . . ."

Discouraged, she had let herself go physically and had put on weight. With her sexual life ruined because of her problems and taboos with men—doctor or husband—she felt powerless and defeated by the fatality of age.

Catherine. 54 years old. Five children, one still at home. She had a good education but never a career. She babies her youngest son and keeps a close watch on him. She often takes care of her grandchildren, and, since they are generally "dropped off" unexpectedly, she cannot make plans for any regular activity of her own. Her parents and parents-in-law, all very old, are an additional burden on her. She, too, has let herself go: "What's the use of taking care of yourself, when you're nothing but everybody's maid?" She seems to take life with a sad, rather masochistic fatalism. She no longer reads, feels she has nothing to talk about but housework, and refuses to seek out her friends who have careers or take interest in her husband's less routine activities. She seems to have grown old, shrunken before her time, and to have given up all social life. Deep down, she is very bitter about it.

Claudia. 55 years old. A farmer. Her eldest son, who helps with the farm, has recently married and lives close by. She has just had a hysterectomy: "They took out everything." Extremely tired and rather depressed, she has had difficulty resuming her share of the farm work and is filled with anxiety as she sees her young daughter-in-law take her place. Her husband spends more and more time at the markets, doubtless chasing after girls. So even "that" will be taken away from her, and since her operation maybe she isn't really a woman anymore anyway. But she is sickened by it and worries about her future. Her mother says she should count herself lucky to be able to retire so early, since she herself had to "slave away and put up with your father far too long."

Claudia says no one seems to understand and that she cannot bear feeling "in the way" before she is old.

These few cases, chosen from among many others, might seem a bit extreme or melodramatic. Most of us women at fifty are doubtless not at their stage, or at least not in the same way. But although the style, the details, are different, the same phenomena and the same questions are present in all our individual life stories.

What do we do when, already painfully aware of our age, we have to contend with the fear of unjustly losing the things life has little by little given us? When our friends chide us, with greater or lesser tact, for those extra pounds, for how we look, for our moods? When our body balks, gets out of whack, needs help? When we no longer feel at home in our skin and think that menopause has something to do with it?

It should be a simple and obvious matter to do something about it. But more often than not, our resolutions to take better care of our bodies or to be on the lookout for changes in our behavior toward others are put off for a later date, just as are our decisions to see a doctor for a routine checkup and to look into our discomforts, minor or otherwise.

The amount of time women spend on themselves, either for need or for pleasure, is minuscule—especially if they have outside jobs as well. Even feeling really sick is not always enough to make us take action, because we are not in the habit of "pampering" ourselves. Other unspoken reasons prevent us from looking after ourselves seriously, as long as it is not urgent: consulting a doctor at menopause amounts to admitting the reality of the problem; in a way, taking it into account makes it exist. And going to a doctor entails all sorts of tedious medical examinations. It means receiv-

ing, whether we like it or not, all sorts of complicated and sometimes contradictory information on how to treat menopause. We
harbor a distrust concerning those hormonal treatments people are
talking about (which is not new—there was already the Pill to
confuse us). And all that costs time and money some of us do not
have or are reluctant to spend.

Then, too, if we do not already have a doctor we trust and feel
comfortable with, it means looking for one. We also fear that thorough tests will uncover some cancer, some defect hidden away
somewhere that we'd rather not know about. We dread seeking
help alone, preferring to take ourselves in hand without bothering
anyone. For some of us, there is a need to talk but at the same time a
reluctance to admit our problems, our helplessness, or our solitude.

Finally, there is the ignorance or fatalism that expects no explanation, no possible response, no relief against the hardships of
growing old.

Who among us does not recognize herself, to a greater or lesser
extent, in this resistance? To face up to one's age and to do something about it require a certain courage. Figuring out the bottom
line on the day of reckoning always inspires fear, especially for
those who up to now have been the most privileged. Not long after
turning forty, Simone de Beauvoir wrote: "My old age was brewing. It lay in wait for me in the depths of my mirror. It was stupefy-
ing, the way it marched toward me with such a sure step, while
nothing within me tallied with it."

But finally, despite all our stubborn procrastination and attempts
to hide our heads in the sand, if we are truly bothered by what is
happening to us, we will end up by taking the first steps to find out
where we are. In order to understand. In order to act.

Let us begin by taking an inventory of the changes that have
taken place, the resources and handicaps of our bodies.

· CHAPTER 2 ·

Physiological Changes

WHILE WE ARE saturated today with information concerning the most frivolous and ephemeral phenomena that do not have the slightest relevance to our lives, we neglect to inform ourselves about what is going on in our own bodies. Very few of us know how the body works, develops, and changes or what its needs might be as we enter this crucial stage of our lives.

If we are ignorant or misinformed about ourselves, how can we *not* be defenseless against the changes taking place within us and their consequences?

Whether we belong to the eighty percent of women who suffer physical distress during menopause or to the fortunate few who report no complaints, all of us should understand our new physiological reality. For sooner or later, we will all pass through this stage in our evolution.

> *Michelle.* 47 years old. Seamstress. Three children. Lives in the suburbs. She came to the doctor about her anxiety and crying fits. She felt dizzy when she lay down; her head often felt heavy, her mouth dry. She thought it might have something to do with her age. Her husband bored her: "He never says anything." He was laid off following an accident at work.
>
> She ended up by saying that her mother's death two years earlier had been a shock and that since then her periods had been irregular. A dispute over the will (although the sum involved was modest) had led to a lawsuit against her brothers and sisters, which was still going on.
>
> At the beginning of the consultation, she didn't know where to begin: her life, her body which was giving her problems, her age, her past. All these things seemed unrelated, with no apparent connection between them.

Many of us have a number of things in common with Michelle: uncertainty as to which of our problems are related to menopause, difficulties in coherently presenting our situation to the doctor, indecisiveness about what to do next.

Many women of our generation have remained extremely ignorant about their bodies. They have had children, probably used contraceptives, enjoyed lovemaking without really knowing how it all worked physiologically. We often maintain an embarrassed or careless distance from the "mechanics" when everything is going smoothly. And today, now that our reproductive role is definitively over, it may be even more tempting to persist in our ignorance of these matters on the grounds that they no longer have any relevance for us.

In this we are mistaken. Our bodies will remind us of how relevant it all is, whether we like it or not. It would have been far easier if we had known in advance, if we had foreseen certain things. But who wants to think ahead to menopause or carefully look into its manifestations and the difficulties that accompany it? Very few, no doubt, but we pay a price for our reluctance. Thus we are generally caught by surprise when our turn comes. We notice without paying very much attention that our periods are becoming irregular, either coming too often or not often enough. They skip a month, come back, get scantier, and then . . . nothing. In other cases, they simply stop, all of a sudden. Naively, we think we may be pregnant—a good way to forget the reality of our age! But the pranks the body plays don't forget us.

During some ordinary night, we suddenly wake up drenched in sweat, as if from a nightmare, and throw the covers back to cool off. After a few moments, everything is strangely normal. Then come other nights, with the recurring sweats that interrupt and ruin our sleep.

In the daytime, we are bowled over by short but scorching desert winds that beat against us and envelop us head to foot, leaving us damp and limp. So that's what they're like, these famous hot flashes that are like calling cards of the change of life! Happily, all this goes unnoticed by those around us, who pay no attention to our odd new habits of suddenly throwing wide the windows, unbuttoning our collars, rolling up our sleeves, tearing off our sweaters, and then reversing the action shortly thereafter.

But it is truly necessary to make an appointment and consult with one's doctor. The minute we feel rising within us this unaccustomed effervescence, the likes of which we have not seen since puberty, there are a number of reasons to see a doctor. First of all, we need to understand the event, to grasp the mechanisms that have been set in motion so that we can cooperate with the doctor in finding a new and satisfactory equilibrium. Second, we need to be assured that it is possible to help the body get over this difficult hurdle, but that any treatment for menopause (if a treatment is desired) requires a complete medical checkup, regular medical supervision, and a choice of medications, hormonal or otherwise, appropriate to each individual case. Third, we need to sort out which problems are related to age and which are not. Many women, overly optimistic or careless, use menopause as a kind of catchall for everything that is not as it should be and assume that time will take care of everything. The doctor will be able to determine what is what and treat the age-linked and other problems appropriately.

Finally, we should realize that the purpose of a thorough examination is not to pronounce us sick (even of age), but to be able to pinpoint our weak points and our strengths. It is in recognizing our assets that we can overcome our liabilities.

• OUR HORMONAL MECHANISMS PRIOR TO MENOPAUSE •

In order to understand what changes will occur in a woman at menopause, we have to step backward and take up the story from its beginnings.

The female child is born with her entire supply of eggs (ova) already stored in her ovaries: some four hundred of them will reach maturity in the course of her lifetime, one ready for possible fertilization every month of her reproductive years starting with puberty. If fertilization does not occur, the body eliminates the unused egg and uterine lining, and again dips into its reserves the following month.

The ovaries manufacture and deliver the eggs, and the uterus receives them when they are fertilized, but there is far more to the story than that. The control comes from a small gland in the brain called the pituitary, which issues the orders that set in motion an entire chain of processes. The means of transmitting these orders are the hormones, substances produced by various glands and released into the bloodstream. The hormones then trigger a relay system which in turn secretes other hormones that finally reach the target, the ovaries to be activated.

The ovarian cycle thus depends on the pituitary, a gland about the size of a walnut lodged at the base of the brain (see figure 1) whose importance is primary, since it controls numerous endocrine functions. In the case of ovarian function, the pituitary controls the secretion of hormones in the ovary.

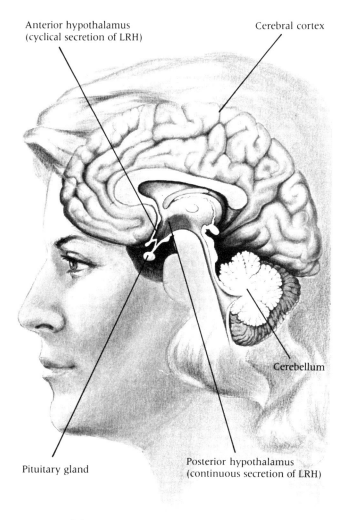

Anterior hypothalamus
(cyclical secretion of LRH)

Cerebral cortex

Cerebellum

Pituitary gland

Posterior hypothalamus
(continuous secretion of LRH)

Location of the Pituitary and Hypothalamus in the Brain

Figure 1

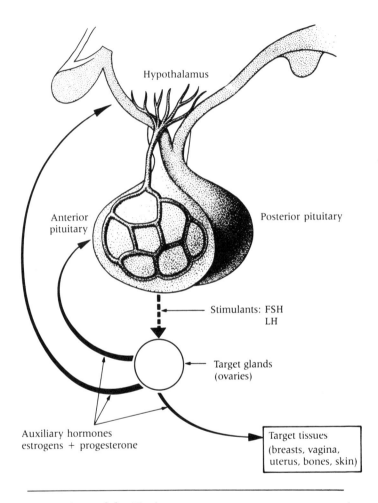

Interactions of the Pituitary

Figure 2

Estrogen is secreted by the follicle (a kind of envelope surrounding the egg). Its role is to stimulate the growth of the uterine lining (the endometrium) each month. There are two main estrogens, estradiol (or, more precisely, estradiol 17B) and estrone.

Progesterone is secreted by the corpus luteum (literally, the yellow body, so named for its color), as the follicle is now called, after ovulation. Its role is to regulate the growth of the endometrium and to prepare it for the implantation of the egg.

In order to control the ovaries' secretion of estrogen and progesterone, the pituitary makes use of two other hormones, called gonadotrophins (figure 2). These are FSH (follicle-stimulating hormone) and LH (luteinizing hormone). As its name implies, the essential role of FSH is to stimulate the growth of the follicle until it breaks toward the fourteenth day of the cycle, expelling the ovum it contains. LH stimulates the follicle's secretion of hormones. It appears that it is the sudden rise of the LH level that causes the rupture of the follicle and ovulation.

But things are actually even more complicated. While the ovary depends on the pituitary, the pituitary receives its orders from the hypothalamus, a small nerve center situated just above it (see figure 1). Not much is known yet about the hypothalamus, except that it is composed of various nuclei (or zones), each of which is in charge of regulating an important life function.

The hypothalamus is the brain of the autonomic nervous system, composed of interconnected nerve cells that transmit ultra-rapid messages. Other messages—less rapid but more durable—are transmitted by active substances which propagate themselves in the form of granules all along the nerve fibers. Through its nerve connections, the hypothalamus centralizes the information that it receives from the body's various chemical and circulatory traffic. All this information, which comes from the outside (pain, for example) as well as from the inside world (our well-being, discomfort, hunger, thirst, sleepiness, and so on), is integrated, compared, and synthesized so as to reach a decision that will be translated into an order to be carried out. Operating beyond our consciousness, the hypothalamus issues orders that govern the entire involuntary bodily system aimed at assuring the maintenance of our life and growth.

The hypothalamus is constantly analyzing and keeping track of a number of processes, including the sugar content of the blood, which keeps it informed on hunger or satiety, and the carbon-dioxide level in the blood, which enables it to regulate such functions as breathing, blood pressure, and muscle tone. On the basis of this information, the hypothalamus controls the state of wakefulness or sleep, the impulses of hunger and thirst, the secretions of the glands (gastric juices, bile, saliva, et cetera), and many other functions. It does so:

· By acting on the blood circulation: The nerve control of the arteries, the veins, and the capillaries all depends on the hypothalamus—this is the autonomous nervous system. It orders vascular constriction or dilation, and consequently controls the blood flow for an entire area of the body.

· By acting on a whole series of nerve relays that control sleep, hunger, thirst, pain, the metabolism of fats, the distribution of fluids, and so on.

· By activating nerves that stimulate the secretion of various pituitary substances, which in turn stimulate the secretion of other endocrine glands such as the adrenal glands, the thyroid, and the ovaries.

The hypothalamus is also an emotional crossroads, a junction between the messages of our conscious brain and those of our autonomous nervous system, the seat of actions and reactions, as can be seen in figure 3.

An external emotion, such as fear caused by an unexpected event, will make us pale, redden, gasp, perspire—all because of this close interconnection through the hypothalamus. It is to this organ that the pleasant and unpleasant emotions caused by what happens in our life, our relations with those around us, and our place in society are transmitted.

Let us return to our more immediate concern, the ovarian cycle. One of the zones of the hypothalamus acts on the pituitary and orders the secretion of FSH and LH through the intermediary of a specific triggering factor called LRH (luteinizing hormone-releasing

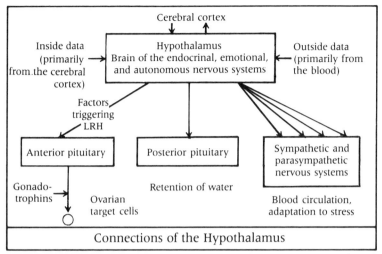

Figure 3

hormone), which activates sometimes LH, sometimes FSH, and sometimes both at the same time. The human being is believed to possess two hypothalamic centers secreting LRH (see figure 1). One fundamental posterior center located in the zone called the median eminence assures the basic secretion of FSH and LH, while an anterior center located in the preoptic zone functions intermittently and is responsible for the discharge of FSH and LH prior to ovulation. The hypothalamus controls the pituitary through the intermediary of LRH. In response to the hypothalamus's command, the pituitary increases the secretion of FSH and LH, which as we have seen accelerates the growth of the follicle and increases its production of ovarian hormones. These ovarian secretions not only act on the target organs such as the uterus; they also act by feedback on the hypothalamus and the pituitary, stopping the secretion of FSH and LH. As a result, the ovarian secretions themselves fall off rapidly. And the cycle begins again, at least until menopause (see figure 2).

The orders for all these actions and reactions come through the bloodstream: gonadotrophins and ovarian hormones are carried through the circulation, while the triggering factors spread from the hypothalamus to the pituitary through small local vessels. Cells have individual receptors for each kind of message, and each receptor is extremely sensitive so as to be able to capture the message from the circulatory system and obey the order received. Figure 4 shows the variations in the blood level of FSH and LH and of progesterone and estrogen during the menstrual cycle.

• WHAT HAPPENS AT MENOPAUSE? •

When the ovaries stop functioning, usually at around fifty but varying according to individual factors including heredity, the secretion of estrogen and progesterone diminishes and their content in the blood falls to near zero. The hypothalamus reacts by secreting excessive doses of the LRH triggering factor, as if it were trying to whip the deficient ovaries into action. The level of the gonadotrophins FSH and LH rises under the effect of LRH (the FSH level at menopause is ten to fifteen times higher than normal, while the LH level is three to four times higher), but the menopausal ovary no longer responds.

So the regulating system we have described no longer works at menopause. There is an imbalance, and the information received is no longer integrated. Is the disruption in the production of gonadotrophins sufficient in itself to explain all the symptoms of menopause? Of course not, but the crisis can spread beyond these two LRH-secreting nuclei and affect all or any of the surrounding hypothalamic centers, producing the wide range of symptoms observed in different individuals.

The specific mechanism of these upheavals may not be known, but the results are there: hot flashes, profuse sweating, dizziness, strange sensations of heaviness, fatigue, a tendency to gain weight, eating binges, sudden variations in weight, water retention, swelling, and other discomforts. And, as we have seen, the hypothalamus is also a point of juncture where our agreeable and disagreeable emotions are registered and integrated.

These emotional conditions are often unfavorable for women during menopause—the very time when the crisis in the endocrine

Action of the Pituitary and Ovarian Hormones on the Ovaries and
Endometrium during the Menstrual Cycle

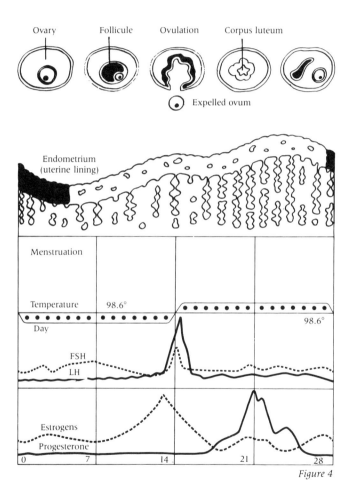

Figure 4

system is in full swing. One wonders if the coincidence of the upheavals in our endocrines and our daily lives may not explain some of the symptoms experienced in particularly difficult menopauses: the sensations of strangeness, of light-headedness or heavy-headedness, the dark moods, depressive tendencies, memory losses, feelings of hopelessness and discouragement, the inability to cope. If so, a favorable emotional situation could help us redress the imbalance.

It is our awareness of the complex interaction between the psychological and the physical that makes it possible to act upon the endocrine system or upon the morale, or upon both at the same time.

• COMPARING PUBERTY AND MENOPAUSE •

Puberty and menopause are the two stages in a woman's life defined by menstruation. At puberty, menstruation begins; at menopause, it ceases. The hypothalamus and the pituitary play a predominant role in both.

At puberty, the pituitary begins to secrete FSH and LH under the genetically programmed impulse of the LRH signal. This programming comes from the hypothalamus, and the result is the appearance of the menstrual cycle and ovulation.

At menopause, FSH and LH are also secreted, but since the ovaries do not respond, they become hypersecretion. The programming now comes from the ovaries, which stop producing eggs.

At puberty, the production of estrogen is responsible for the appearance of secondary sex characteristics, which develop within a relatively short period of time, from eight to twenty months. The onset of menstruation follows by about a year.

At menopause, estrogen activity ceases rather abruptly, but the regression of the secondary sex characteristics is only partial and occurs over a number of years.

At puberty as at menopause, there are important differences from one woman to the next. At both stages, women have to confront and adapt to hormonal changes and their consequences. Physical as well as psychological changes must be accepted and integrated. Women must say to themselves: "This new body is mine," and everybody does not accomplish these mental gymnastics with the same flexibility. Some find it relatively easy; others find it extremely painful, strange, and disturbing. But when they have overcome the ordeal, they are the stronger for it. They have acquired a new dimension.

• THE STAGES OF MENOPAUSE AND THEIR DURATION •

Since menopause means the definitive end of menstruation, it occurs at a precise month, generally around the age of fifty. Nevertheless, we cannot use the word accurately until a number of months later, when it is certain that menstruation is over for good. This uncertainty leads us to use the term "perimenopause" to encompass the months of menstrual irregularities preceding menopause when the situation is not yet clear.

Before the cessation of menstruation, there is a long period, sometimes lasting several years, when the woman approaching menopause notices discomforts ranging from minor irritations to more serious difficulties. These are all the more disturbing for the woman who is not forewarned and who is therefore constantly worrying about what is happening to her and what she ought to do. This uncertainty and lack of information are extremely preoccupying and draining. Whom can she ask? How can she recognize what stage she is at in her body change?

Concerning menstruation, the warning signs are irregularities in the cycle: variations in quantity, periods that are either too close together or skipped entirely for two, three, or four months. Sometimes there are clots in the menstrual blood.

Concerning the body, the breasts are often tender, disagreeably sensitive to the touch, and even painful. The stomach is more distended at the approach of menstruation, and there is unaccustomed fatigue, especially during the second half of the cycle. Other symptoms include irritability, anxiety, sleep disturbances, diarrhea or constipation, and a touch of sore throat. The signs vary from one woman to the next. This period can spread over several years.

Not all the changes that take place are attributable to menopause. Nor do they all occur in each woman, or all at the same time or at the same rate. In some, the changes are telescoped, taking place within a few months or even weeks, especially following a shock or as a result of excessive worry or stress. In others, they extend over several years. We can assume that the more concentrated and intense the process of change, the more energy we will need to confront it.

Some women are able to take these profound biological changes in their stride. Once again, it's different for each person: not every puberty is turbulent, not every adolescence is crisis-filled.

But for the majority of women, it is not so easy: eight out of ten women in France experience physiological discomforts directly caused by menopause: dizziness, fatigue, migraines, and the various other physical ailments that precede or follow the inescapable cessation of ovulation and menstruation. These are not only "weaklings," or women who have nothing else to do but complain of their woes. And yet one continues to read that these problems— concrete enough to leave us drenched, exhausted, or pale with insomnia—are "subjective," that is, unverifiable by others. True enough. One can not always summon a hot flash in the doctor's office to show they exist.

As if to buttress their claims that women suffering from menopause are "whiners," the moralists add that African women, who can not afford to pamper themselves, do not have these problems. While this remains to be scientifically proven, one can only ask if it is really possible to make such a comparison: in most Third World countries, relatively few women live to reach fifty, so the problem all too often does not arise.

What we do know statistically is that the women who suffer most from aging and menopause come from the most economically disadvantaged or culturally deprived segments of the population. And it is precisely these women who most lack information on how to alleviate their difficulties.

Who is at fault, then? The woman who lets herself go, who gives in to her problems, or the society that creates the conditions least conducive for women to confront this critical time?

There is, of course, a predisposition in the endocrine system of each individual woman to secrete in greater or lesser quantities the various substances that give rise to these disruptions. We can be relatively unreceptive or highly receptive, but we cannot escape them. Nor can we be expected docilely to go from sufferer to Wonder Woman.

Naturally, there are those who delight in parading their physical problems. There are also those for whom this age coincides with other problems, aggravating already difficult lives. There are those, too, who pamper themselves because no one else does.

There are a thousand and one ways to go through menopause. One can be discreet about it, resigned, prudish, hysterical, triumphant, ignorant, turbulent, depressed, courageous, cowardly, or quite simply oneself, the same as always, the way we were before, the way we will be afterward. An entire gamut reflecting our differences, but all in response to the same perfectly objective reality.

But most of us live through this gray cloud with a kind of shyness and even shame, with little comfort and no consolation. Which is why we wanted to share this delicate time in a woman's life.

· CHAPTER 3 ·

Society's Image of Women at Fifty

THERE IS NO denying that our bodies change. But the changes are far greater internally than they are on the surface, and if we consider our bodily mechanism as a whole, they are very limited. It is also possible for the changes to remain more or less invisible and discreet, and for our daily lives to continue as usual. Possible, but very rare.

In most people's minds, it is not pleasant for a woman to reach fifty. Menopause is supposed to be a handicap, a difficult hurdle. Society does not know how to react to women at menopause, what to do with them, what to do for them. It is as if this partial change calls into question the totality of a woman's roles and her emotional and social place in the world. And society, even while perhaps regretting that a woman must leave behind her traditional functions of seduction, motherhood, and service to others, gently but speedily steers her toward her new fate as an "old woman" Western-style: "demoted," pushed to the background, or in any case occupying an ill-defined place in a society of short-term production and reproduction. That's how our immediate future is erased for us. The story of Janine is a case in point.

> *Janine.* 49 years old. Divorced, two children that she raised on her own. She is a pretty, smiling woman, extremely well groomed, and works as a receptionist at the headquarters of a large firm. Sometimes she accompanies visitors as an escort/interpreter. She enjoys her job because of the variety of people she meets and likes the people she works with.
>
> The personnel manager has just told her that "another position would be more appropriate for her age." At first she protests that she is in excellent health, but she soon understands that the point is to reduce her visibility, given the public's reputed preference for young women. For Janine, the sudden realization of the injustice based on age is a devastating blow. Until then, she had been confronting menopause with optimism and without notable physical discomfort.

Even more painful than what is actually happening inside us, then, is the hurtful and discouraging echo sent back to us by the outside world.

It is not really in our power to manage this new phase of our lives as we see fit. As social creatures, we are tied to the fate of the human collective, which interferes with our most private affairs whether we know it or not. No matter how far removed we may feel from those who came before us, no matter how autonomous and independent in our relations with our contemporaries, in countless ways they exercise an immense power over us.

We are weighted down with a mass of preconceived images and ideas concerning our roles and our fate. These notions are even more threatening to us than actual encounters with the few "bad cases" of tormented menopausal women which, however, infrequent, serve to confirm prevailing prejudices.

At this time of our lives, when biology and our personal history intersect, we become the symbol of something that goes beyond the eddies set off in our immediate territory. Even if those close to us accept us with our changes, we are suddenly feared, avoided, nullified by society at large. What ill omen does a woman's menopause bring to unleash such aversion, such fear? Are our wrinkles, slackening flesh, and gray hairs so very different from those of men our age? Why does public opinion find us so much more repellent?

And sometimes, even frequently, this deterioration is more imagined than real and visible. Many women today do not show their age, either physically or mentally. Their vitality is obvious, their charm certain, the quality of their relations with others tempered by maturity. But, as soon as their age is *known*, they are not looked upon in quite the same way.

What people cannot tolerate about women at fifty—the reason they are avoided—is that they serve as an unwelcome reminder of the precariousness of the duration of human life. As Simone de Beauvoir noted, "Every society tends to live, to survive. It exalts the vigor and fertility linked to youth. It fears the weakening, wearing down, and sterility of old age." Old age is still far off, but menopause is nonetheless the specific, irreversible biological event that signals powerlessness to transmit life.

Given that female fertility represents a struggle against death, could it be that there is some deep-rooted, atavistic repulsion, a collective reflex of self-defense against those who give up this struggle? Ever since the dawn of time, a whole mystique made up of expectation and magic fear has centered on this impudent power of woman—her fertility. Could it be that, as soon as her childbearing ability ends, as soon as she is shorn of this power, there is a temptation to turn with impunity against her? The revenge of man, jealous but dependent on the womb of woman. And, for our part, a carefully orchestrated education has succeeded in making us swallow whole hog the maternal personage and its virtually exclusive roles. "Nature" gets the blame—a convenient justification for a situation rigidly maintained by a social system set up centuries ago. Even today, if women have attained some position in society or professional life, their roles are almost always secondary or subordinate. Their "power" is still prudently channeled into the family.

If our usefulness is seen as synonymous with our physical fertility, what are we when we are sterile? What good are we? And, after fifty, sterile we will all be, leaving behind what society sees as our essential calling. Even if this change is only symbolic, even if we have long since stopped wanting to have a child, in menopause we are propelled out of the production circuit linked to motherhood.

It is hardly necessary to dwell here on the power of the stereotypes dealing with women's roles. Innumerable studies and contradictory declarations address the subject without having in any way shaken the citadels of traditional thinking. In order to justify our existence, not only do we have to bring children into the world, we have to take care of them afterward, not only for their sakes, but to prove that we are good for something. When they leave us, the entire edifice of our purpose in life risks collapsing, without any help in sight. The result for some is a premature aging: it has been noted that menopause occurs earlier in women whose children have left home.

As if all this were not painful enough, must we be made to pay for it by the merchandisers, who cleverly exploit our fear of being shunted off with the old folks through well-tuned advertising campaigns designed to precipitate us toward a frantic race of rampant consumerism? We are all the more vulnerable in that, throughout our lives as women, we have been bombarded by the cult of ideal beauty. We are expected to continue galloping after the fashions that would have us skinny one year, a bit rounder the next, paler, suntanned, ravishing behind our typewriters, provocative while washing dishes, svelte while pregnant. They count on our conformity to keep us running after the unreal "norm" presented in women's magazines—that we will keep on trying to resemble those idle, ethereal-looking models who frolic about in incongruous settings—

and to convince us to change yet again our makeup, clothing, and accessories. And all in order to please, please, please—or to be less displeasing to ourselves.

Needless to say, it is not enough to be eternally young. One has to be beautiful too, because youth and beauty are the combination that wins happiness. Next we are shown that beauty and youth can be bought. And women's magazines abound to forewarn against the slightest change wrought by aging. One reads: "Looking younger than one's age is an art we must begin to practice early," or "Avoid being competitive: a woman who is tense wrinkles earlier."

In such a context, as we watch ourselves aging, how could we help but feel in Simone de Beauvoir's words, "the shame of being more or less ruined and of growing inexorably farther and farther away from the ideal of humanity"? Playing on our desperate wish to conform to the ideal, it is all too easy to cast out a net and haul us in.

The advertising media ceaselessly hammer away at us, repeating that this diet, this formula, this product will enable us to slip into the perfect skin. The mirage of these magical promises sucks us into the dream, even while it is stressed that *good* results cannot be achieved without our efforts: if we fail, it can only be our fault. So here we are, guilty of aging.

We are fair game from the moment this familiar body seems threatened. Those who stand to gain from the advertising hype know what they are doing, and they are going to flush out the money wherever it is, from any pocket. The cosmetics industry manages to flourish even during the gravest economic crises. For middle-class women, there are beauty creams, partial or complete facelifts, fabulous treatments, and specialized magazines selling hope through costly but miraculous remedies.

For women of more modest means, skeptical or unable to afford such expense, there are the weight problems given wide coverage in the women's press: "To be thin is to be young." One has to eat "better"—which naturally costs more, but popular morality can more readily accept additional costs for food than for luxurious ointments. But if you are employed, try following a reducing diet in the company cafeteria. Try summoning the strength, when you are tired in body and mind, to pass up a second helping or another dessert, which seems to compensate you emotionally or with energy for the expenditure of yourself. Age increases lassitude and especially the time needed to recover one's strength. So there goes your figure! Those extra pounds most women pick up after menopause make the simple act of buying clothes complicated and depressing: we scour the stores to find a size 16 or 18, often available only in gloomy colors and severe, impractical styles.

And then women are taken to task for their frivolity and "narcissism"—after absolutely everything was done to awaken and exploit their fears of aging. What bad faith to turn these feelings against them! Magazines aimed at women must stop acting as accomplices to a destructive ideology. And do the advertisers realize that what they are selling is sadness and defeat?

We have no intention here of maintaining that it is as pleasant to be old as it is to be young, or that it makes no difference. We fully agree that beauty is a marvelous source of pleasure: from time immemorial art and love have found in it inspiration and passion. And youth carries with it a hope none of us could do without.

What we are saying is that, whatever pleasure we take in contemplating and admiring youth and beauty, we cannot allow them to constitute our sole purpose and entire love of life. What revolts us is not these qualities in themselves, but their inflation by modern means of exploitation. Youth and beauty have ceased to be mere sources of pleasure and admiration and instead have become the be-all and end-all, commodities to envy, commodities for sale. Worse, they have become attributes without which one has no right to a place in the sun.

As long as we are mentally and physically healthy, it is only natural that we should seek pleasure in living. According to a report by the French National Foundation of Gerontology, "The aptitude for pleasure and the capacity to create situations that make such pleasure possible are criteria for normalcy. . . . But if the environment makes it impossible to create these situations, what must we conclude? In short, we must take into account both the individual and the society in which he or she lives. Which brings us to the need to try to define the criteria of sickness in a society."

So we find ourselves trapped in the illusory norms created by our society, and the slow but relentless advance of age can make this mad quest for the impossible dramatic for some. If a woman's entire self-image is bound up in such mythical perfection, impervious to the effects of time, how can she bear it when this perfection recedes ever further? Obsessed by the ideal image one has to imitate in order to be accepted and loved, what can she do but, at best, "put up a good show" or, in despair, lash out against herself and give in to self-disgust? It is a great pity, and a great waste.

Where do we draw the line between necessity (looking after one's body and appearance) and the beginning of a secret alienation? At what point does a healthy attention to self—both normal and pleasurable—become anxiety, obsessive fear, and even nightmare?

We weren't born yesterday, but still we let ourselves be manipulated like novices. How can we resist the onslaught? How can we maintain our sense of proportion and humor? Perhaps by telling ourselves that there are too many of us in the same boat to continue letting ourselves be pushed around. By persuading ourselves that we have nothing to do with this dewy-eyed Body Perfect imposed on us as the ideal.

This model may have impressed us at one time, but today we would like another more in keeping with our reality. What kind of woman are we going to become in our change? Where can we find likable representations of women over fifty in this world of the omnipresent image? Certainly not in films, posters, advertisements, or art photos. The public does not care much for this "intermediary age." Two rare exceptions are the actresses Simone Signoret and Ingrid Bergman, who dared break the taboos by showing in close-ups the reality of their age and their features—and with what presence, what human impact!

On the other hand, why did they have to "touch up" the mature beauty of the French philosopher Simone Weil on her campaign posters when she ran for public office? Why this exaggerated "face-lifting"? Is the voting public to be politically directed by

some seduction lever? Do female candidates have to be "kissable" to inspire confidence?

Isn't "beauty" a broad enough term to include women whose lines bespeak intelligence or humor, faces whose very ugliness has a charm in itself? (It should be noted that our present obsession with youthful beauty did not always hold sway. Museums are full of portraits of women of all ages, and these portraits—which make no effort to camouflage the marks of time—once decorated walls.)

Not only do we not exist as faces, silhouettes, smiles, or glances; we are also absent from dramatic portrayals of love. This tacit prohibition suggests to us the incongruity—even the indecency— of our wish to be desired and desirable, the preposterousness of the very notion that men could be touched by our autumnal charms. This attitude is well illustrated by the recent outcry that surrounded the French film "Corps à Coeur" ("Body to Heart") which showed realistic love scenes between a middle-aged woman and a young man. The film was called "indecent" and "disgusting"— such unaccustomed prudishness in our open society! In the absence of real or fictional role models—since women our age are either not depicted at all or are somehow ridiculous in advertising and films—how can we visualize ourselves, define ourselves, affirm ourselves?

It is daily life that offers us a mirror: friends, family, the streets, the workplace all bring us face to face with women our age. How do we experience this? If we let ourselves fall into the cruel trap of reducing women to mere appearance, we will doubtless feel anxious, hesitant before this reflection for fear of discovering there a reality at odds with the sought-after dream.

The spectacle of our own aging on someone else's body is not always easy to bear, especially since every mark of time's passage is practically an offense, a weakening of the surrounding collectivity. It could be tempting to flee this reflection of a face that is no longer acceptable and scarcely has the right to be seen. Or, if we are lucky, we may know how to look with friendship and tenderness on these traces of life's weight in another, and how to read in them the resources they signal.

Despite the overriding importance attached to how people and things look in our Western civilization of appearances and glitter, we do not have to reduce ourselves to a facade. We are not window dressing, all the more pathetic for its artificiality. We have other, deeper dimensions. We can hark back to the female role models of our childhood and youth, which have had a far more lasting impact.

What impressions have we retained of these women in their declining years who people our memories? Perhaps a face, but also words, a way of being there, of speaking or remaining silent, of suffering or smiling, of making us want to follow their example or avoid it. We were influenced by a certain way of living and thinking, by values arising from our childhood milieu, itself part of a larger social group inserted in a moment of history.

If we who were born during the 1920's and '30's want to understand the kinds of issues facing us today, we should turn our attention briefly to the historical context that shaped who we are. We spent our childhood before World War II, and, as soon as it ended, we were thrown into a new economic, political, and cultural world. Most of us were brought up according to principles and under conditions that were later profoundly disrupted. We have been either witnesses to or participants in changes we have not always been able to gauge, and from which we have not necessarily known how to benefit. Living in a period of transition, we sometimes waver between two worlds, two often contradictory value systems.

As women, undoubtedly more vulnerable today as we go through menopause, how do we experience the broader societal changes which perhaps compound the disarray brought about by our own bodily changes?

We sometimes feel disconcerted by the freedoms claimed by our daughters, but at the same time we reject the still-recent submission of our mothers and grandmothers, and deplore what we fear may be our own.

Before, a brief and discreet sexuality was all that could be hoped for. Today, sexuality is shouted from the rooftops with its freedoms, its mechanics, and its problems.

Before, a woman had to have children to justify her femininity. Today, the birth-control pill has changed the rules: love can be free, and women want to seek their meaning outside of motherhood.

Before, we had to bow before the supremacy of men. Today, the validity of the concept has been demystified, and young people are seeking new ways of relating to one another that are no longer based on allegiance and inequality. It is a struggle, or a quest, to which "older couples" are not always accustomed. Even if the young have not made much headway with these problems, at least they expect to come up against them.

Our generation had to submit, too, to the power of our elders: mothers, mothers-in-law, and other all-powerful women. But now it is necessary to call into question the traditional hierarchical rights in a balance of power that is reversed, and sometimes to defend ourselves against the "terrorism of youth," individual or collective.

Our generation was expected to assure the continuity and to pass on time-tested knowledge and values. What is required of us now is to question, to doubt, to innovate, and to know how to adapt to change.

Our generation had to resign itself to old age, sickness, and death, or to find meaning in them. Today, the tendency is to deny them, to flee or disguise them, and the duration of life itself is prolonged in a new reprieve. Modern grandmothers have other faces and other roles than those of our childhood—faces and roles which have now been relegated to the great-grandmothers.

Each of us can add to this list of comparisons between our past and our present. Are we the winners or the losers? What is certain is that we are often torn between the claims of these two worlds which overlap, cancel each other out, and are mutually stimulating. It is up to us to find in all this something for ourselves. We are in a position to redefine our future options so as not to let ourselves be caught off guard, manipulated, and duped in these changes, like the victim in the following tale.

The story takes place about forty years ago in a small convent. The nuns live in undisturbed tranquility, each day like the last, until the bishop announces his visit. Great excitement and a flurry of preparations. The Mother Superior defines to each her place: "The old nuns, because of their fidelity and long years of piety, will have the place of honor and be presented to His Grace." Young Sister Jeanne, a bit disappointed but obedient, devoutly helps prepare the meal in the kitchens, dreaming that one day, perhaps, her turn will come. Many years passed, and the little convent was so well behaved and trouble-free that no one at the bishopric ever thought of coming to visit it. Then a young and dynamic bishop arrived in the diocese and decided to give a boost to the religious orders. He announced his visit to the convent, which had just received some novices. Great excitement and a flurry of preparations. The Mother Superior defines to each her place: "Needless to say, these new arrivals, on whom the hope of the entire order rests, deserve the encouragement of His Grace and will be presented to him." Sister Jeanne, now old, will not be there for the celebration. Cheated, but obedient, she will devoutly help prepare the meal in the kitchens, with a sigh.

We must not let ourselves "be had" as this poor woman was. We live in a world where change can finally play in our favor. To a great extent it is up to us to slow it down or speed it up, but it is not easy for women of our generation to forget our upbringing or to hold up under the weight of the present opposition to the changes we all more or less aspire to.

Our way of life has been profoundly altered, even while parallel changes have not taken place in the traditional structures and ways of thinking. As a result, we are too often trapped in our roles—in our idealized and fixed image—even though we know that the days of women's "inferiority" and powerlessness are more or less coming to an end. The age of fifty is almost inevitably a confrontation with these contradictions, calling into question our very identity.

> *Irene.* 51 years old, married to a senior executive. Five sons, of whom two are still adolescents. She is so depressed that it is her sister who brings her in for the first time. Her expression is dull, uncertain—the kind of gaze one finds in people who don't know where they are anymore. The sister speaks

first, expressing her disgust at how Irene is treated by her husband, who uses a disparaging tone when he speaks to her at all, which is rare since she has put on weight, aged, let herself go. The sons imitate their father. Irene listens to all this, passive, mortified.

Medically, there is little to say. What Irene needs especially is to talk to someone who listens to her. Being without a career, she believes she has served as a nursemaid and feels used. "My parents told me that all I had to do was marry and have children. But, when that job is finished, what are you good for?" "I resent my husband, but he has his reasons, too. His parents idolized him."

She added that, for the men in her husband's family, it was a tradition, and indeed a point of honor, that their women could (and must) remain in the home.

· CHAPTER 4 ·

A Renewed Identity

WE CLING TO our identity with every fiber of our being. It encompasses everything from our physical image to the deepest levels of our psyche, everything that is visible and expressed as well as everything that remains unspoken but continuously evolves, unseen, around an unchanging core. Identity crises can be triggered by major bodily and life changes—puberty or menopause, unemployment, a divorce, the loss of a loved one, retirement—and by the shocks and ruptures these changes provoke. A crisis is an acute and painful moment in an evolutionary phase, but it also implies a dynamic movement toward another, more stable situation.

This precious identity is like a jigsaw puzzle composed of thousands of pieces that have been painstakingly assembled, though without our knowledge, ever since childhood. The pieces are fashioned in the image of the significant figures of our emotional life (whether we have chosen or rejected them). They are modeled by our experiences, the happy or sad memories that we have stored away in our unconscious and sorted out or reconstituted according to our preferences, though not the less unconsciously. From this unceasing work is constituted the original, precious, fragile ensemble of who we are.

The body has its place in this identity, as do our family background, and our social milieu. And we have the uncertain freedom of adding the last word, that is, of making all this into something that is peculiar to us. If, in this unique whole which includes our health—some element is destroyed, lost, or damaged, the image cannot be reconstituted as it was. When one has the feeling of losing oneself, even to a limited extent, the result is anxiety or even distress.

So if today we vacillate between our nostalgias and our fears, with a sense of being unconnected and alienated, we feel alone and abandoned. How can we maintain our taste for the present or future when we feel so ill defined, as if we had lost or denied the outlines of our very self? This is how two out of three women experience the psychological problems of menopause. Some can put up with them quietly and overcome them on their own; others suffer so acutely that they need help.

Lucy. 51 years old. A professional pianist. She came in after reading an article in a family-planning magazine advising women to discontinue the birth-control pill before menopause. She suffers from hot flashes, which disturbs her psychologically.

At night she awakes with a start from nightmares, with painful, inexplicable, and totally unknown physical sensations unleashing anxiety attacks that keep her awake for hours. She has feelings of confusion and dispersion. During the day she feels an uneasiness, a strangeness; she has the impression that everyone is hostile to her. She thinks she might be on the verge of a depression, but panicked at the mere idea of seeing a specialist. It took her several months—terrible months for her—to make up her mind to seek help from her regular doctor.

We all have had difficult moments where some passing cloud darkens the aging process. Such moments enable us to understand what the most seriously afflicted women go through. They also focus our attention on the need to seek better ways of maintaining our overall equilibrium during this pivotal period of our lives.

The loss of equilibrium and feelings of strangeness have numerous and subtle causes. They can be internal or external, recent or of long standing; they can accumulate and proliferate if conditions are favorable. There is no inflexible determinism that dooms us to the misfortunes of this difficult age, but, if we want to be at our best, we may have to fight on several fronts.

The woman who has the good luck to be spared these problems is not abnormal, any more than the woman of the same age who suffers terribly and whom we cannot ignore. Since it is impossible here to present each individual's story, some women may find these lines too negative. Others may think they fall short of the problems they themselves experienced. Our hope is that we may succeed in reminding readers of their own experience and help put it back into a context, thus making it easier to handle whatever difficulties may arise.

Among the external difficulties, we have already seen the prevailing aversion in our Western societies toward aging in general and women's aging in particular. There is a school of thought that sees the discomforts and problems of menopause as a largely cultural phenomenon, varying from one country to the next in accordance with how women in the particular society perceive their roles, their aging, and the effect it may have on their status. But although it is worth our while to assess our societies' cultural oppression, which unquestionably compounds nature's effects, we must take care not to get bogged down in this awareness of the environmental factor and fall victim to it. Shedding light on this facet does not always help: it is possible to concentrate on our conditioning to the point that feelings of inevitability and powerlessness to escape are accentuated.

If it is important at the collective level to rebel against this type of cultural tyranny, it is also necessary, at the individual level, to understand where it hurts us and what we are resisting, and then to take practical measures of all kinds (as we shall see in the second part of this book) in order to alleviate, come to terms with, or turn to advantage the consequences of aging.

Our culture is not the only element responsible for whatever physical and psychological discomforts we may be experiencing at this time. A number of influences come together simultaneously and become entangled in a crossroads we must traverse in order to find ourselves again later—a bit the same, a bit different.

Hormonal changes—the sudden "power failures" or "overloads"—play a role in our changing self-perception. As we have seen, menopause triggers in us an endocrinal disorder. The hypothalamus, the seat of our emotional life, is subjected to new stimuli which it then transmits throughout the system. We react more or less strongly according to whether these neuro-endocrinal exchanges are anarchic or discreet, and depending on the stability of the psychological structure that receives the repercussions. We have probably already experienced the influence of our hormonal life on our personality and moods during our menstrual periods or following childbirth.

The tendency toward mood changes is an integral part of our being in that it is linked to our physiological system. It gives us our emotional flexibility, the flashes of intensity in our perceptions and imagination, the wide range of our innermost feelings. The richness of our personality is there. Men are often thrown off balance by this psychological makeup which is so different from theirs, and since they do not know how to follow the iridescence of our feminine nature, they become hostile.

So these fluctuations, being neither understood nor accepted, are turned against us. Women have to repress them and suffer the psychological consequences of such repression. Other women flaunt these mood swings because they are *supposed* to be part of the feminine personality. During menopause, when everything tends temporarily to get out of proportion, our behavior can become exaggerated and take the form of whining, self-pity, or an aggressivity unbearable to everyone.

To avoid both denials and caricatures, we can learn how to recognize the warning signs of our changing states. We can learn how to go about maintaining our moods within the limits of our mental comfort (and that of those around us) without blocking or unsettling our fluctuations. Finally, we must learn not to be overly fearful of what lies in store for us in the coming years.

The hypothalamus is not the only biological culprit; a disrupted thalamus is also partially responsible. The mental picture we have of our body, which enables us to recognize ourselves with a certain accuracy and permanence, is organized within the gray nuclei lodged in the thalamus. This capacity for symbolization is an extremely important mental function. It is what makes possible the affective process of identification, that is, the overall organization of our own identity, which controls our way of relating to ourself and others.

Above and beyond these effects on our relational life, if the mutations in our chemical processes cause us to lose, however slightly, the precise contours of our image of self, our perceptions will become distorted. The slightest variation in our appearance is relentlessly tracked in the mirror, aggravating the fears of aging which have insidiously taken root. We then have the tendency to exaggerate the changes, whether permanent or temporary, that are in fact occurring. Physical and mental causes become intermingled and confused.

For some time now we have all experienced mornings when we just didn't have the heart or energy to face the day, or when the mirror confronted us with puffy eyes and features rumpled by a bad night. In the past, we could always hope that the morning hours or a little cold water would wipe away the traces. But today we fix the image, no longer expecting time to take care of things, and we speak of "physical deterioration." The danger of these morose encounters with ourself is that we begin to confuse our dark imaginings with reality. Our features and body become subordinated to this unhappy self-image: we abandon our body to its fate, our face frozen in a tense and joyless mask. Summoned before its time, old age is ready to settle in for good, if we allow it.

Given the close connection between our physique and our psyche, any loss of value in our body image, for whatever reason, can call our entire identity into question, with serious repercussions for our overall equilibrium. Will we have the same perceptions of our reasons for living, our goals? What will happen to our capacity to love and be loved? What will we ask of ourselves, what will others expect of us if we are no longer the same woman? A host of questions, both vague and specific, loom up. Our ability to adjust to these changes will depend on how we have directed our goals and aspirations up to now—in short, on where we have concentrated our power.

Our psychological stability and our relationships with others are in large measure linked to how we feel about ourself. Yet the women of our generation are torn between the need to be in harmony or at peace with ourselves—the need to *like* ourselves—and what amounts to a cultural and even religious prohibition against seeking our own needs. We were taught that we had to "forget ourself" in order to prove we loved others. Even Freud wondered if there were not an incompatibility between self-love and love for others, between "narcissism" and "altruism."

"Narcissism" is one of those ambiguous words that trap us between disapproval and desire. Most often, the word is confused with self-centeredness, with "having it all my way." But self-esteem is in no way at odds with love for others. In fact, the opposite is true, and we need to love and respect ourselves. It is impossible to reach out to the other if we start from nowhere, that is, from a self that is denied or is in fragments. Narcissism and identity are inextricably bound together, and all through life they share a common fate, since narcissism plays such a vital role in the continuity of our identity.

Our narcissism is under assault during this period from many quarters. It is the fear or awareness of physical or social decline; it is feeling someone's eyes on your wrinkles; it is when people give up their seats for you in the subway. It is the position given to a younger colleague, the roving eye your husband develops. But, at the same time, our narcissism is what gives us the security that enables us to believe and hope that we are loved, that enables us to play a recognized role in our social environment and thus retain our zest for life. If this security is challenged or denied us, or if we have doubts about it, our self-image and our plans for the immediate and distant future will be seriously affected.

But we can learn not to confuse the whole and the part: we do not have to be devastated by the loss or change of a certain *aspect* of ourselves. We have a lasting core which assures our continuity, whose essence is unchanging even while we shed the old forms and roles we have outgrown, even while the shape of our future begins to come into focus.

Another piece of that puzzle we call our identity is the "ego ideal," which is related to our narcissism and gives it its dynamism. In general, each of us has developed an ideal image of self as a young and active adult. It is an image that little by little we fear we cannot live up to. How can we project a future ego ideal if we are still stuck with an outmoded self-image? Our physical and mental persona is controlled by our expectations and demands on ourself and our awareness of who we are. We feel good about ourself when the gap between what we dream of being and what we really are (or think we are) is tolerable. This not always peaceful coexistence between the image and the reality—the desire and the possibility—has been subject to a certain number of tensions ever since childhood. But what can our relation be today with this body in the throes of visible, palpable, and hidden metamorphoses?

Every bodily or relational change we think we can attribute to the aging process affects our sense of wholeness and hence our identity. It is only natural that this would create in us perplexity or even a depressive reaction: withdrawal is a normal response to loss of security. In fact, withdrawal implies an ability to see reality as it is and take it into account. Even if we have to step back—to take a kind of distance from ourself and others—this will enable us to set out once again toward other horizons, other visions of ourself. What is involved, then, is not so much a loss as a redistribution of energy, turned toward the self or toward others. The fifty-year mark can thus be one stage among many in the life cycle.

Another way of reacting is to become aggressive. This, too, is a sign of vitality, but it can be painful. We catch ourselves espousing emotionally charged, outrageous, or sweeping judgments concerning ourselves or those who, for better or worse, play important roles in our emotional or active lives. Forgetting the ground rules of nuance and compromise, we will inevitably feel victimized by these fallings-out, believing ourselves undervalued, persecuted, misunderstood, hateful, or contemptible.

Then all our energy turns to aggressivity, and we strike out willy-nilly in all directions, punishing ourselves without cause or attacking those around us with whatever means we have at hand—our weapons, our masks, and various forms of blackmail. These may take such forms as the conscious exaggeration of our discomforts in order to pressure and worry those around us, stated or unstated demands which exceed the other's resources (emotional, sexual, et cetera), and playing on the weaknesses of our partners in order to dominate or harass them or make them feel responsible for all our problems.

By giving in to these aggressive tendencies, we are sowing guilt feelings in ourselves and others whose harvest will be misunderstanding and conflict. Such behavior is a sure sign of a bruised and suffering ego, of which we ourselves are the primary victims. More than ever during this unstable period, we have to recognize the ambivalence and multiple realities of every individual, and that these changing states of mind do not compromise our deeper coherence. Our maturity escapes us at the very moment that our body underlines it.

Just as animals are touchier and more fragile during the molting season, so also are our character flaws, our latent "neuroses," more likely to rise to the surface during menopause. We thus have also to contend in this difficult period with our more or less resolved conflicts, with psychological frailties buried in our unconscious, born of the struggles of our earliest childhood for the autonomy of our desires. We are particularly vulnerable if those around us do not show patience and tenderness, if we do not have a recognized and acceptable (to us) place in our environment, if all our own resources are exhausted or inaccessible, or, finally, if our body betrays us.

One of the classic psychological reactions to anxiety, sadness, or boredom is to smoke, eat, or drink for consolation. By a twist of fate and to our misfortune, it is precisely at this time of our life that the appetite center is subjected to hormonal shocks, sometimes to heightened stimuli. The fruit of this unhappy collusion is an irrepressible appetite leading to additional pounds forbidden by both fashion and medical advice, resulting in a new source of anxiety or guilt, to be forgotten, naturally, in food or drink. Yet what could be more normal than this movement toward the self, this effort to secure at least *this* much reassurance.

More than ever, we have to try to understand ourself, to place ourself in our life's context. Each age has its limits, and we have to know the limits of ours. Each of us must ask the question, "What are my limits now?"

The limits of my power of sexual seduction: in this area, our dark broodings can play us a bad turn far more than the objective reality. It is all too easy to interpret the definitive end of one's menstrual period as proof of the ultimate loss of femininity, even if hormone therapy results in monthly bleeding. And if the fear that one's sexual life and desires will change takes root, a lack of responsiveness may arise—the bitter fruit of one's pessimism.

The limits due to a now ineluctable sterility: this reality will be particularly painful for single women or for married women who wanted children but never had any.

The limits of my physical strength, which I can perhaps no longer take for granted, limits that may express themselves in muscle, bone, or other pains.

The limits of age, if I am looking for a job, or if I want a job with greater responsibilities which are more likely to be entrusted to younger people, who are expected to have fresher ideas.

And, in another mode, the limits of time. Menopause marks a step in the chronology of my life. Will the weight of experience cause experience to lose its novelty? Will I have the enthusiasm and sense of expectation needed to build a future whose contours I can barely discern?

Will I be tempted to forget that I may have another thirty years or so to live—years whose quality in terms of activity and fulfillment will depend largely on me? It would be unrealistic, as well as self-defeating in the extreme, to minimize these long years of maturity ahead and concentrate instead on the miseries of an as yet far distant old age.

Menopause is a kind of mental and physical initiation rite ushering in a new stage of life. In the midst of it, one sometimes wonders if the past can give any meaning to the future. When everything looks bleak, it seems as if all these images stored in my head—all these experiences, all this learning, all these relationships—are totally useless in terms of helping me to go on participating in the world and in life. What is the good of all this left-over experience? And then, perhaps my heart is not yet resigned, despite the wear and tear of the years. Perhaps no memories—either happy or painful—have yet been able to dry up my expectations and desires, and I sometimes find myself seized by impulses and yearnings that are not "appropriate" for my age. What can be done about this double identity: the chronological age inscribed on my driver's license and the state of my subjective sensations, desires, and fantasies? One day I feel older than the hills, another day young and sprightly, and sometimes I simply live without thinking about age at all.

Those who witness my doubts, my ravings—what can they think? And how important is what they think? Is this transitional age a kind of betwixt-and-between of our emotional life, a falling between two stools? It is an awkward position and forces us to make a choice.

Either I react, get hold of myself, and, if necessary, seek outside help, or I let myself go. If those around me push me or go along with it, or if my body gets out of sync, or if I give in to its imbalance, I run the risk of living in a state of anxiety, depressed and morose, and of deteriorating. Will I be ashamed—or afraid—to become one of those women popping pills and tranquilizers or tied to the psychiatric couch?

Men, too, have their periods of vulnerability, which differ from ours. But they are in a better position to cope, because they can channel their energies into their outside lives, their professions and the social activities associated with them. But many women do not have an "outside life"—they often do not have jobs and are not involved in a cause or even sports or distractions. And if their children are grown, they cannot rely on them—luckily for the children!

Many of those who do work have demeaning jobs, which, far from enhancing their lives, are actually an additional burden on their dual roles as women. Above and beyond bearing up under the exigencies of the human condition, women throughout their life are called upon to take on roles and duties that are often crushing, dispersing, contradictory—and which go further toward explaining their difficulties than any supposed constitutional weaknesses.

Psycho-medical circles traditionally believed everything could be explained with the catchall label "female hysteria," which soon became pejorative in everyday usage. Menopause only accentuated this morbid tendency. Freud's disciples were long reluctant to attempt to shed light on the landscapes of this dark continent. Thus, women have not been helped with their specific problems, which in any case are not reducible to a simple explanation.

This does not mean that some women do not wallow masochistically in their problems without trying to resolve them on their own. Certain women think their symptoms are unique and experience this "uniqueness" as a kind of guilt, branding themselves as "neurotic" and either brooding on their woes or exploiting them to attract pity. Others in this category do seek help, but follow whatever treatment is prescribed haphazardly without really believing in it, thus dooming it to failure.

In our era there is less and less tolerance for the passive acceptance of physical and mental ailments. Scientific progress coupled with health-care programs and medical insurance have created new demands, instilling in the public the idea that health and the suppression of pain are *rights*.

There are many ways of approaching the various treatments of mind and body that are available. One is impatience, insisting on

immediate results obtained almost magically. Another is dependency, the indiscriminate and passive yielding to psychologists or doctors and drugs—the latest prescriptions or remedies—without the kind of involvement that makes treatment effective.

Finally, there is participation, making the effort to understand the causes of the problem so as to be able to weigh the possibilities for available treatment. This requires perseverance, discernment, and discipline, because what is taking place inside us is not simple; it is not always quantifiable, regular, or predictable. Nor should our change of life be seen as a private affair to be borne in solitude and silence. We will gain greatly by approaching it in partnership with others concerned: our spouse, friends, doctors, and other women

Happily, a great many women have the courage to confront squarely the psychological difficulties of this period and to seek their causes. In fact, in our profession we are struck by the fact that such women—those who dare to question themselves, both individually and in group sessions—are in the majority. While most are perhaps less willing to call into question society's overall structures and institutions, they do not hesitate to challenge their own personal beliefs and habits, to face up to their own limits and dig into their pasts in the hope of changing the present or of discovering new possibilities.

The so-called "weaker sex" has less reason than men to be fearful of losing face or privileges. On the contrary, we gain in the process. Less dependent than is generally believed on protection and security, women as they grow older know their resources and how to trust themselves better.

If our psychological makeup is solid and we have managed to hang on to our zest for life, we can hope to emerge from this period of uncertainty, marked by crises and faltering questions, with a more positive attitude toward ourselves, a better sense of who we are, and better equipped to get the most out of life.

CHAPTER 5

Relations with Others

WHATEVER NEGATIVE ATTITUDES society at large may have toward women our age, on a personal level most of us are backed up by an entire network of family and friends who hold us dear.

The years we are living today are probably those in which we are most concerned by the things happening to those around us. Whether these are good or bad or simply everyday things, we are *involved*. We generally feel a responsibility toward several generations: our children, either still with us or nearby; our elderly parents who rely on us; our peers—spouses or lovers, brothers and sisters, friends and colleagues—who are all perhaps more subject than before to various worries and problems which indirectly affect us because of our relationship to them. Time has wrenched us from the egocentricity and carelessness of youth, and all these things touch us now.

Women our age are the first to be informed whenever anything happens. We are the ones who listen, give advice, help, and organize the support system of family and friends with the efficiency that comes from experience. The presence and quality of our relationships with those around us lend color to these years. Because our emotional equilibrium depends on our sense of being loved, respected, and useful, we can get some notion of the distress of others for whom this sense is lacking.

> *Marie.* 49 years old. Lives in the suburbs and does not drive. Her two sons have already left home. One is in the army. The other is a student in the city, who comes home only to have his laundry done and to extract some money from his mother, for whom he shows no consideration.
>
> Her husband travels a great deal and says his wife is "not much fun to be with" these days; for the past two years she "always has an ache or a pain somewhere." "It's her menopause," he concludes with impatience, and leaves again.
>
> Marie is unhappy, given to feelings of emptiness and disappointment about the "ingratitude" of her loved ones. She says she would like to go back to work but is too shy to take the necessary steps. She has no real sense of physical aging and still has a lot of energy. But how can she channel it?

Thus, it is in relation to others that we are led to take stock of our lives, like the sorting out and rearranging we do—with pleasure or nostalgia—at spring housecleaning. With or without the help of those close to us, the time of reckoning has come which will enable us to envisage aging and the future. Are those around us a kind of hell? Or are they our life's blood, our reason for being? Whatever the case, our "spiritual menopause" will depend in large measure on what takes place between them and us.

For those of us who are married, our need for emotional support generally focuses on our spouse. If we are aggressive or whining in our demands, he will be on the defensive, refuse to hear, come back with his own demands, or simply fail to understand that what his wife needs of him is a boost in her self-confidence. As a result of this misunderstanding, there will be disappointments, irritations, or worse.

Incomprehension and powerlessness to respond to the needs of the other in an ever-widening gulf between the two partners can lay the groundwork for divorce: a recent study by the U.S. Census Bureau projects a divorce rate of twenty-four percent for women between the ages of fifty-five and fifty-nine. It goes without saying that women are only partially responsible; above and beyond the conflicts arising from deteriorating communication, middle age often coincides for each partner with a personal crisis which can only aggravate the situation. For the wife, it is menopause. For the husband, especially if he is a professional, it is the point where he is expected to have achieved something in his career. While she may be wrestling with problems of womanhood, he may be facing job insecurity or disappointments to his self-esteem, or he may be throwing himself headlong into his work as an escape. If the partners cannot or will not share their respective anxieties and concerns with the other, the gap between them cannot but increase, and it is not difficult to imagine the disastrous results for their union.

The man, who is aging as well, may also be taking stock. No longer able to bear the recurring frustrations of his existence, he may be directing his interests outside the family, seeking other compensations—social, sexual, or romantic. The years may have taken their toll on the relationship for both of them, and the woman's response to this situation will depend on the extent to which she can or cannot imagine being self-reliant, for example through a career.

Happily, not all relationships run aground on the mid-life crisis. Some couples even find a powerful sustenance in the face of external difficulties. It is nonetheless a particularly harsh test, compounded by all sorts of delicate circumstances—the situation and health of one's parents, the state of one's professional life, the age of one's children. Much of a couple's success in weathering the storm will depend on the habits they have already developed in the past for resolving their differences and on their ability to distinguish between the trivial and the essential. It is in this way that each partner can surmount his or her personal difficulties without aggravating those of the other. The pleasure of growing old together is to try to do so in the best way possible—with humor, compassion, and complicity.

There are also those who live alone, especially unmarried women. Twenty-six percent of all American women between the ages of forty-five and sixty-four are single, widowed, or divorced. Germaine Greer has noted that insecurity is the bogeyman of those who fear freedom. But the fact is that the freedom ascribed to single women—and for which they are often envied—is purchased ever more dearly as the years go by. According to the director of the International Health Foundation–France, "To judge from the case histories, it would seem that unmarried women are up against not only the usual problems associated with this period of life but simultaneously with additional problems associated with the temporary loss of self-confidence, all the more difficult in that it is not compensated by the regular presence of a long-time companion who has been aging at the same time. There is also the crucial fact of not being able to share problems with a partner who has known you for a long time. The woman on her own finds she must, perhaps even more than the married woman, take care not to let down her guard and always give the appearance of being in top form."

Given the present norms of family life, one of the most powerful relationships—heavily freighted with diverse emotions—is that between a woman and her children. Mother–child feelings evolve over time, but they remain central to the woman throughout her life.

By the time most women reach menopause, their youngest children are approaching adolescence or already in it. The oldest have left home and have often become parents themselves. It has been noted that the presence of children still at home affects the way a mother goes through her menopause. While it does not eliminate whatever physical difficulties she may be experiencing, having young children very often lessens the nervous and psychological repercussions of menopause and can even retard the actual cessation of menstruation.

Young women today are having fewer children and compressing their childbearing years, which means that they will be younger than we were when the last child leaves home. For their sakes, let us hope that they will have found a purpose in life beyond an excessive and exclusive devotion to their families, thus providing for their long years of post-maternity.

Too many women of the generation now reaching fifty have staked absolutely everything on their roles as mothers and suffer from feelings of emptiness, powerlessness, and purposelessness after their children's departure. Some feel cheated, as if all they got for their sacrifices was the distance from their children—a distance that appears to increase if the mother was possessive or controlling. Too often in the past, and perhaps still today, the value of "devotion" was exaggerated and the sacred union of the tight nuclear family glorified. When everything explodes, these abusive and abused mothers are left with the painful sense of having been victimized, and weep over the ingratitude of their loved ones.

It can be a stroke of good luck to have adolescents still at home at this time. Youngsters bring a breath of fresh air, a sense of renewal. There is movement, discussion, stimulation. Young people do not like to see their parents—especially their mother—grow old and do everything in their power to keep it from happening.

They also afford a new input, new ideas. If the house is open and the youngsters are sociable, other adolescents will be around—adolescents who often turn to us for guidance and support, with us tempering and complementing the role of their own parents.

In other cases, the relationship is stormier. Mother–daughter relations are particularly delicate, especially if the girl's puberty coincides with the mother's menopause and if each is strongly affected by the event. The result is tension, hostility, and family guerrilla warfare, with disagreements between the parents concerning how to raise the child and how to handle the situation. It is difficult to assess whether the mother or the daughter is more to blame for the rivalry, the mood swings, the sudden outbursts, the obstinate refusals of each to understand the world and the values of the other. The greater the age gap, the more bitter the struggle and the more difficult it is for each to accept their differences.

The relationship with an older son or daughter often entails having to deal with their romantic or sexual involvements, more or less explicit in keeping with the parents' tolerance. Sexual freedom, especially for girls, is more often than not a concession the parents make, however reluctantly, to the moral standards of the times, without really recognizing the positive aspects of this freedom or knowing how to act toward it.

The sexual freedom of young people can provide a variety of reactions. For women who fear the loss of their charms, or who have never dared or wished to have a relationship with anyone but their husband, the spectacle of a young person's pleasure (which they believe to be too "easy") can be irritating. Other women vicariously live vanished adolescent loves through their daughters, acting as accomplices and helping them avoid the father's jealousy. However the situation is handled, the feelings that are aroused are often compounded by the critical gaze of neighbors and grandparents.

If the children end up getting married in the traditional way, which is what usually happens, the woman will have to become a mother-in-law with grace, discretion, and the ability to maintain the often difficult balance between speaking out and remaining silent that must characterize healthy relations with the young couple. We watch and, if need be, do what we can to help these young people start out on their careers and adjust to their lives as new parents. Most often, it is the woman who offers assistance to the younger generation (which sometimes can deteriorate into a form of exploitation).

Thus, when children leave the nest to embark upon their own lives and start their own families, the mother can feel—according to her way of seeing things—either that her family has disintegrated or that it has become enlarged. The same holds true for how she sees her role. Women our age act as a link to whom the generation ahead and the two behind look for help. We remain the daughters of the youngest generation's great-grandmothers who are still alive and we are ourselves the grandmothers of the children of our sons and daughters. Do we see this as an enrichment or a burdensome multiplication of tasks?

If we want to take pleasure in our role as grandmother, it should be on our own terms. We do not want to squeeze ourselves into the mold of earlier times, nor could we if we wanted to. But stereotypes of grandmothers—which no longer correspond to the modern women we are—die hard, especially among young children and adolescents. They still dream of us with snowy hair, bent over our knitting in rocking chairs by the hearth—unless, more cynically, they imagine us in our dotage or at everyone's beck and call. Even if we must disappoint these expectations, the reality is that a great many of us, by choice or obligation, are active women following careers, with all that implies in terms of lack of time, struggle, and fatigue (but also in terms of being in touch with new attitudes and lifestyles, with what is going on in the world). The fact that many young people still conjure up such outmoded visions of grandparents undoubtedly corresponds to an implicit expectation of availability and tolerance—which should give their parents food for thought! As for us, we can find quality time to establish privileged relations with our grandchildren, especially since we are freed from the responsibilities associated with raising them while they in turn are freed from the hostility arising from the Oedipal bond, reserved by definition for their parents.

When grandchildren frequently drop by their grandparents' house, it generally denotes a healthy relationship between the parents and grandparents. This is not always the case, however. It can also indicate a severe emotional dependency, where the grandchildren are used by their grandparents as substitutes for the parents, who go along with the situation to make up for their own guilt at having left home. Once again, we see the negative effects of the close-knit nuclear family and the power of certain women, specialists in emotional blackmail, who cannot let go of their compulsive role of mother hen. Naturally, we never recognize ourselves in such a description!

On the other hand, many women are happy when their children are finally able to stand on their own feet, feeling they have "put in their time" and no longer having the energy for the task. For them, it is a sign that their efforts to teach their children independence have borne fruit. Now that they are free—or almost—they can finally look a bit to their own needs and think beyond the confines of the family, even while not entirely letting it go. All this takes place gradually and subtly as the woman seeks to find the "right distance" which suits everyone.

Even as the responsibility for our children lessens, there is often another which grows heavier with each passing day: responsibility for our parents, most often an aged mother who confronts us with the spectacle of either the cruelty or the dignity of old age. To flee their old age, these very old women frequently dredge up from the shadow that old game of identification between them and us. In our youth, they were our model; today, they look to us. They admire the dynamic and young (everything is relative) women they see in us. Even while they continue to criticize and find fault, they envy us for the fact that we are still full of life and try, pathetically, to emulate us.

If we have not managed over the years to achieve an adult distance from our parents, we will again fall under their influence, whether they are living or dead. We will take up their rituals, adopt their vision of things even if it is no longer appropriate to our time. The past will be more attractive and have a stronger hold over us than the present. In such a case, it is pretty certain that our relations with our contemporaries and with young people will not be very dynamic.

If, on the contrary, we have succeeded in achieving a measure of adult autonomy, we can freely draw on our parents' experience, their values, whatever suits us today in preparing our future. We can have a tender thought for those of our mothers—or the mothers of others—who taught us a taste for life and how to struggle against adversity, and who made us see that it is possible to enter old age with courage, gaiety, and love.

When our parents have died and we become the oldest generation of the family, it is we who become the link with what the past represents in terms of social anchoring, stability, and continuity. We will become the family archives, the repository of memories, the codes of the family clan. We can speak of the sidelights of history as we lived it, the world of our childhood, not to mention the family folklore. And if that dates us, too bad! The generations that follow will sooner or later also need to know where they come from.

Theoretically, women our own age are in the best position to understand and help us. But how much sympathy actually exists among us? How much solidarity? Misogyny seems to be rampant among women as well as men. The fact is that the identification we spontaneously and involuntarily feel at seeing the face of a woman our age too often triggers not compassion or solidarity but a mean-spirited rivalry armed with a deforming lens.

One finds women who would never admit to not feeling well, especially to another woman, or who exult in having managed to pass time's obstacles lightly and scorn others from the height of their security. They repress the symptoms of menopause and pretend they do not exist. They pour their entire energy into their "duties"—family, career, social life, politics, the church—and refuse to allow the physical or psychological discomforts of menopause to stand in the way of their activities. They then point to themselves as an example and accuse those who suffer of pampering themselves. Happily, such women are a small minority. If we are among them, perhaps we should try to moderate the triumphant air which is so painful to others our age.

We have to recognize that, despite all the efforts of the women's movements, "sisterhood" remains a myth. The hostility among women, who have lived as rivals in relation to men, sometimes reaches its height in the workplace, where individualism—which has always been preferred by those who benefit from it—only aggravates the situation. Young women workers, for example, wage a nasty war against "the old girls," who in turn go overboard with heavy-handed references to the value of "experience." Some of the older women, meanwhile, either from cowardice, conformity, or rigid adherence to the "way things have always been done," sabotage the efforts of the younger women to introduce changes (legitimate or otherwise) into the workplace. Against such a background, it is hardly surprising if the older women, instinctively seeking to protect themselves from snide comments or worse, conceal whatever depression or physical discomforts they may be having or, alternatively, convert them into somatic symptoms and become truly and seriously ill.

Nonetheless, while setting up workshops within the context of France's 1971 law on the provision of continuing education in the workplace, we have had occasion to see that a number of young women are sensitive to the difficulties of their older colleagues (perhaps because they remind them of their mothers), asking for the formation of group sessions to deal with their adjustment problems. Leaving aside the somewhat patronizing and condescending aspect of this initiative, it is noteworthy that, for some young women at least, female solidarity is beginning to prevail over the generation gap.

In all our relations with young women—daughters, daughters-in-law, friends, co-workers, those involved in the same cause, or even those we meet in the street or in stores—we must take care not to act superior or arrogant or to throw our age at them like a privilege. We must not lose sight of the fact that our greater age, which we sometimes perceive as a disadvantage or mark of inferiority, can as easily be intimidating to younger women, who see it as a threatening superiority. Some young women say outright that they dread women of fifty. One of us still remembers her own thoughts about these mature women when she herself was young: "They seemed to know everything, referring to facts I didn't know. I was afraid of what seemed an evil power. They were such large presences, filling up the whole space. I was afraid they would devour me, win me over to their side, as if I would become one of them before my time and against my will."

Since the 1960's, however, the balance of power between the generations has somewhat reversed itself and the all-powerful hold of adults over youth is greatly diminished. Without becoming passive victims, we should strive in our relations with the younger generation toward an equality of exchange and a spirit of mutual recognition—which means we would be true to ourselves without being either rigid or fawning. Young people hardly appreciate those "mature" adults who try to hop on their bandwagon, using the same provocative language, spouting their ideas, and adopting their fashions. Such pathetic attempts smack of hoax and demagogic mystification, and it is painfully obvious that what we see here is less a matter of connecting with youth than of fleeing oneself.

If we do not want to live in isolation either nor or in the long run, we must carefully cultivate and preserve the balance of our relationships with others. The better our social integration, the less will we have to suffer the problems connected with the onset of old age. And we must not forget that this depends in large measure on ourselves.

> *Jeanne.* 54 years old. A "mother" in a home for needy children, she has raised fifteen orphans from two different family groups.
>
> She is round of face and body, with twinkling eyes, humor, gaiety, and straight talk. She says she is far happier now than she was as a young single woman casting about for a direction in life.
>
> When she takes stock, she sees the road already traveled: "her" children have been able to overcome the sometimes serious problems connected to their difficult starts in life. The oldest are on their own. They have found work and love. "Not bad!" she says. For her, a bit of respite and her own projects, but not yet. She still has four children to raise.

· CHAPTER 6 ·

Relations with Doctors

WHILE THE NATURAL PHENOMENON of menopause cannot be reduced to a strictly medical dimension, we do have to understand its mechanism in order to maintain our good health during this period. A doctor we trust, either man or woman, working in partnership with us can help us through our menopause, although we do not intend to reduce menopause to its strictly medical dimension. It goes without saying that a doctor who sees the patient as a kind of helpless ward under his guardianship, who has only to "leave everything to him," is to be avoided.

One need not be sick in order to consult a doctor. A body in the throes of change must be relearned. The knowledge that we gain from talking with a physician will be a precious tool for managing our health and our aging.

If, by the age of fifty, we do not have a doctor, we have either never been sick or we have not found one who meets our needs. We expect a great deal of doctors—sometimes too much—or we have expectations they are unwilling or unable to meet. They are neither saints nor magicians. Medicine has its limits. And doctors, being human, have their limits too.

Even if our expectations are reasonable, we may have to shop around before finding a doctor who suits us and who feels at ease with us as well. A doctor will not refuse to help, but the quality of the relationship goes beyond all rules or obligations, and the freedom of choice is ours. It is a question not merely of technical issues to be dealt with, but of an interpersonal relationship with all its subjective aspects. And menopause, the change of life, is not a neutral subject for either the patient or the doctor.

Everybody knows that most general practitioners are overworked and that few have time to spend more than ten minutes talking with the patient before moving on to the examining room. This is especially true with women in our situation. It is all too easy to dismiss us as whiners or hysterics who baby ourselves or dream up unverifiable problems with an eye toward reaping benefits from our condition.

Many male doctors dread consultations with women of fifty for a number of reasons. One of us remembers how, as a young medical student, she heard the remarks of her teachers or their medical assistants about women around fifty who came in for headaches, depression, and fatigue. She found their sarcastic, stinging comments worrisome and perplexing: "On the one hand, I respected these eminent physicians who were teaching me clinical medicine, and I was eager to learn. On the other hand, I vaguely sensed their prejudice against older women. I identified strongly with the women even while promising myself never to be like them. I wanted to tell them: 'Stop exaggerating! Tell them the truth about what you feel and they'll believe you more.' At the time I had no notion of psychosomatic medicine and the doctor–patient relationship, and I naively believed that the doctor was always objective, impartial, and in search of a real, scientific diagnosis."

Many doctors cannot bear hearing complaints they do not understand: whatever falls outside the scope of their university curricula is not admissible as evidence. And since they do not know how to cure these symptoms, they feel a kind of hostility toward those whose complaints are incoherent and contradictory (to their ears) at the physiological and anatomical level.

The reasons that a doctor feels irritated when confronted with the grievances of a menopausal woman are complex. Aside from those just cited, the doctor can be said to be disconcerted by menopause as by any psychosomatic symptom.

Moreover, a man is still a man even if he is a doctor. If he is thirty, the fifty-year-old woman who consults him will be about his mother's age; if he is thirty-five or forty, she will be just an older woman. Whatever the case, she is no longer young at a time when he is interested in those younger than himself. A particularly unhappy incident occurred to a fifty-three-year-old woman consulting a young gynecologist for treatment of her menopause and who was forced to hear: "I'm sick and tired of these old biddies who want to get laid up to their seventies!" The woman stormed out. One can hardly blame her.

The doctor who is the same age as his patient may be having his own problems with being fifty. Unless he is a wise man or blessed with a superior intelligence, the tendency is there to differentiate himself from a person his age who speaks of fatigue and depression, of fears of aging and no longer being attractive. The practice of medicine confers, of necessity, a certain sense of power. It is therefore easy for a doctor to recoil from seeing a resemblance between himself and this woman who suffers from her aging in his presence. He still wants to remain young and vigorous, not necessarily from narcissism alone but in order to exercise his profession. To categorize her as a hysteric or an unbearable nag is the easiest solution.

The patient may remind a young doctor of his mother. If she handled her menopause well, he would tend to be encouraging—

he would have a good model to offer. If, on the contrary, his mother had a difficult, depressive menopause, he might feel sorry for his patient and want to help, or he might dismiss his own ambivalent feelings with: "They're all alike! Let's get this over with as quickly as possible."

So it is important to choose a doctor we believe can meet our needs and expectations, and the doctor–patient relationship will develop gradually throughout the period of consultation. We cannot expect everything the first time, and one has to remain within reasonable limits: the doctor has more than one patient a day. It is advisable to ask beforehand how much time is available for the first meeting, to prevent oneself from being hurried or maneuvered. And if the doctor's availability and readiness to listen is important, so is a careful clinical examination, both gynecological and general. Whatever worries the patient has should be mentioned to the doctor, and if everything cannot be resolved in the first consultation, a return visit should be scheduled.

Above all, one must be able to trust one's doctor, and it is here that the preliminary choice is important. A doctor's skill, concern, friendship, intuition, and perceptiveness increase tenfold when a woman or man comes to him with confidence, an open mind, and attentiveness. Real confidence can only develop over time, but from the very outset one must believe the doctor is competent and open to one's problems, and then judge him by what he does. There must be a respect on both sides. This is true for all medical consultations, but especially for those involving women at this delicate age, who come seeking not only relief for a particular problem but also reassurance, to get away from society's negative prejudice concerning menopause.

It must be noted that there are two kinds of medical treatments: one for the rich and one for the poor. The symptoms described by a senior business executive are more credible than those presented by the menial worker. By the same token, complaints from a man are listened to differently than those from a woman.

Even when the top experts of the medical world turn their attention to menopause, it is to express the hope that we will grow older with grace and dignity. Like swans on a lake! This is laughable, not at all how we see ourselves. Is this to say that, left to ourselves, we would go through our menopause with an indecent vulgarity? Such words are undoubtedly meant kindly, but to our ears they are so outdated and condescending as to be totally out of place. How we intend to lead our lives concerns us alone. For the time being, what we are asking of doctors is that they listen to us, inform us, answer our questions, and through their skills help us get through this stage. What we do with all that afterward is our business.

What we have trouble dealing with are the doctors who refuse to take us and our medical questions seriously. We are not asking for miracles, but for help in using to the utmost what is possible and predictable.

> *Christine.* 54 years old. An attractive woman with a successful and demanding career, who has to be at her best to pursue it and to live up to her reputation. She was careful to anticipate the physical difficulties of menopause and follows an appropriate treatment.
>
> She nonetheless finds that her memory is less acute and her attention span shorter. She wants to know if it is possible—and if so, how—to delay these effects. She has heard a great deal about "gerontology" and the science of aging, but the doctors she has talked to so far do not seem to believe in it as a long-term possibility. Given her healthy appearance, they all laugh in her face and tell her she doesn't need anything. So now she is looking for a doctor who can tell her what is possible, what is hopeless, and what is wishful thinking. She has not yet found anyone. She begins to wonder if medicine involves health or only sickness, prevention or merely attempts to repair the damage.

With age, we learn not only how to live in the present but how to anticipate the future with a clear mind: our hope is to add not merely years to our life, but life to our years—and doctors should be able to help us.

Vivian. 51 years old. Mother of seven. A very beautiful woman. Someone came in with her because she considers herself fragile. She assumes a rather pathetic tone. She says she has become so unsteady she does not recognize herself.

She began to have hot flashes two or three years ago, along with dizzy spells, palpitations, and persistent and serious insomnia. Everyone around her was afraid for her, she said, particularly her "very good" husband, a well-to-do businessman. She had an electrocardiogram because of her chest pains, but no abnormality was found.

Six months later she came back and said she was very, very ill. She had had convulsions, but was told it had nothing to do with menopause. She wanted to know if there was any correlation between the two phenomena. The attending physician said there was none and that he was against hormone therapy in any case. The gynecologist then wrote to him stressing that the disturbances she was suffering had begun at the same time as her hot flashes and menstrual irregularities, and that her problems could be favorably influenced by a hormonal treatment. He never answered.

This exceptionally beautiful woman—the mother of a large family, not poor—timidly confessed that she feared the judgment of her regular doctor and that she did not dare go against his opinion.

Time passed, and she returned for a gynecological consultation. The convulsions were poisoning her life. She decided to undergo hormone treatments, and took upon herself the responsibility of giving it a try. It is still too soon to know the results, but at least she insisted on making the decision herself.

· CHAPTER 7 ·

Sex and Love

JEAN-PAUL SARTRE once wrote that there are sexualities that thrive on unfulfillment, just as there are those based on fulfillment. Even if we do not make sexuality the central theme of our lives, we situate ourselves, consciously or otherwise, in relation to it. Whatever our age, we cannot deny the presence in us of this vital yet at the same time fragile urge.

A harmonious love life is not easy to achieve at any age. It can never be taken for granted or arrived at once and for all. Because of the physical changes we are undergoing around the age of fifty, and especially because of what these changes represent psychologically and socially, we have to distinguish between what are real effects on our sexual and love life and what are merely preconceived notions.

If the sexual impulse were merely a matter of hormones triggering the desire to make love—a simple transmission of appropriate signals to the male—the loss of estrogen that takes place at menopause should put an end to this kind of exercise once and for all. But, as we all know, this is not so. Even if some women choose to withdraw, it is far from being the case for all.

To a certain extent, the biological changes can have an adverse effect insofar as they suppress certain hormone stimulations linked to various phases of the cycle. But were these so important in our love life before? Wasn't our arousal a function of many other factors, which can remain unchanged: our partner's interest and desire, his approach, our feelings toward him, and the quality of our imagination which in itself does more to stifle or stimulate our desires than all our glands combined?

The Kinsey Report noted that the duration and stability of sexual desire in women is less threatened by age than in men who fear impotence. Thus, for both men and women, fears are more formidable than reality. But why should these fears be stronger at our age?

What has become of this experience—both intimate and fragile, sensitive, secret and private even in its need for another since it addresses first and foremost our own fantasies and perceptions? Are we more threatened and without resources than we were yesterday? Or, on the contrary, are we better equipped to understand and control what happens to us in this domain?

Sexual activity at fifty, like many other aspects of life, is simply a continuation of what existed in the past. We embark upon this new phase armed with our personality, our state of health, and our libido, and there is not any foreordained reason for what was good to deteriorate, any more than there is reason for what was bad to improve.

Unfortunately, in a number of cases there is a deterioration. Women who had an unsatisfactory sex life in the first place blame their age and see it decline still further. Their sex drive disappears completely, their sexual contacts become less frequent, their pleasure rarer than ever. "I no longer want him to touch me" or "It has become a chore for me" are frequent refrains. But in such cases, isn't age an alibi for refusing sex without joy? If the past is littered with numerous sexual disappointments and failures, it would be difficult indeed to go on with a normal love life.

On the other hand, there are women who experience orgasm for the first time at fifty and over, particularly those who lived in terror of getting pregnant and feel liberated by the end of their fertility. It can also happen when a woman takes charge of her life and develops autonomy, goals, and aspirations for herself, when she begins relating to her partner in a new way, or when she decides to find other partners and this leads her finally to pleasure. Within each human being, no matter how depressed, there is always the hope of something better, of finding once again a taste for life, the warmth of a body, the surge of desire

Our sexual life will stand a greater chance of retaining its vitality if in the past we have enjoyed happy hours of tenderness and love. Still, it cannot be denied that even with harmonious couples, even with generally fit and healthy women, there is sometimes doubt, indecision, or lack of interest.

What, then, are these new obstacles to our full sexual realization? Are they brought about by our age, or by the *idea* we make of it? Or by how others may react to our "pretense" of not wanting to retire our desires and hopes?

This last is an important point. There is no question that the old sexual taboos, prohibitions, and silences that stifled our sexuality as children and adolescents return with a vengeance where aging women are concerned. The strength of the earlier taboos, undoubtedly instituted because of our fertility or approaching fertility, shows us that the beauty of youth alone is not sufficient to authorize opening the gates of pleasure. Then and now, what we see at work is the old social ethic that seeks to regulate for its own ends the sexuality of individuals, the antediluvian moral code that admits no other purpose for sexuality beyond procreation—which reduces our lovemaking to the utilitarian instinct of the animal world.

Many religions have legislated on the rights and duties connected with sexual intercourse. Women with Catholic backgrounds will undoubtedly recall the time when most contraceptive practices were outlawed in the name of the couple(!) or a—however hypothetical—respect for life. The celibate clergy advocated abstinence in marriage rather than pleasure in love for its own sake. Since that time, both couples and women have distanced themselves somewhat from these shackling laws supporting higher birthrates. But even if we have managed to put them aside, haven't they left traces, at least in some of us, buried more or less deeply in our consciousness? The command linking sex and procreation has been so strongly inculcated in some women that the very risk or possibility of pregnancy, even through the armor of contraception, may somehow have justified throughout their entire married lives the pleasure of making love. After all, they were still potentially fertile. Was it the wish to have a child, or the duty to have a child? With such injunctions, could it always be clear?

If we are still unconsciously in the grips of this archaic need for justification, do we feel we have the right, now that there is no longer the possibility of fertility, to enjoy pleasures henceforth without "purpose"? And without the right to such pleasures, how can we feel attracted by them? And do we feel desired by our partners for ourselves alone, rather than for the fertility of our wombs? These are thoughts worthy of the Dark Ages. They have no place in our era of concern about overpopulation, when contraception has been developed and improved. But can we forget that we are the first generation to know the efficient methods of regulating birth? We may have had ambivalent feelings about these procedures, as we perhaps still do concerning the hormone therapy designed to treat the ill-effects of menopause. The collective unconscious, imbued with the prevailing laws, is stubborn, slow to evolve and adapt to change. Its seeds have taken deep root in us, sometimes leading us to listen to and repeat words and concepts that have become absurd.

Given this mindset, we can at least find comfort in the fact that from the teleological point of view our fertility *must* come to an end, our ova *must* be exhausted since they were increasingly altered by the aging process. Psychologically incapable of renouncing the procreative function in the love relationship, we condemn the love relationship to disappear. It has been said that maternity will continue to be, by its absence, the cornerstone of our alienation. Fortunately, not all of us have fallen victim to this heavy conditioning, and in making love we are perhaps, on the contrary, relieved of fears of untimely pregnancies and of having to worry about contraceptives.

There are also women who reach this stage in their lives with the notion that gray hairs make it indecent to continue a sex/love life. This puritan mentality, outdated but nonetheless still widespread, can crystallize into a reluctance to have sexual relations. Such reservations in turn will bring about a restraint in showing tenderness and a holding back of excitement, thus assuring a diminution of pleasure. This will immediately be interpreted by the woman as confirmation that it is no longer "right" to have sex at her age, that she no longer has enough vitality or sufficient hormones to make love. From now on, she will prevent herself from showing tenderness or desire—if, that is, any desire manages to filter through, given her attitude.

Another aspect of the taboos that inhibit our right to a sexual life are those implicitly imposed by our children. At the risk of appearing overly "Freudian," it is much easier for the young generation of adults or adolescents to resolve their conflicts if they are no longer under the shadow of lingering Oedipal desires, if —under the pretext of decency or fastidiousness—they can throw a thick veil over their unconscious image of their mother's body, forbidden but still desired in that unconscious, and thereby push her aside and strip her of her power. They would finally be free for their own loves, without the disturbing reminder of the pleasures their mothers may be pursuing.

Leaving aside the family, where do we find our contemporaries depicted as desirable and desiring women? As already mentioned, we know that with certain rare exceptions women or couples our age are not shown in erotic or pornographic films and books, since our society does not consider us capable of arousing desire. Setting aside, for the moment, the dehumanizing nature of pornography, do we find this situation normal? Why? As women in this age group, where do we situate ourselves in our own erotic fantasies and desires? Is there a blank? Out of our bodies and outside time? Or freely and vividly?

What effects can these commonly held negative judgments concerning our rights to a sexual life have on our sex drive and self-image? Are we capable of loving and making love, of confronting our own body without sometimes feeling discomfort and embarrassment?

If we can answer these questions (which sooner or later age will force us to ask) with honesty, we will have the measure of our capacity for autonomy, our self-confidence, the strength of our libido. What encounters between age, desire, and the image have we experienced?

I look at myself in the mirror: that's me all right. The same as before, the same as always. The one who was twenty years old not so very long ago, with her dreams, enthusiasms, and desire to jump into life feet first. But life followed its course, and wrinkles appeared. My hair, eyes, chin, mouth, stomach, thighs—everything is the same and yet no longer quite the same. A chunk of life has passed; a family was born and grew up. But my zest for life is still there somewhere, in the shadows. It wants nothing better than to emerge, brand new—provided there is someone to receive it, who will not ridicule it.

We make love with our heart and with our body *as it is.* If we run after a vanished dream, wanting our body to be as it once was, we will find nothing but disappointment and regret, and desire will evaporate. If we have no desire ourself, there is no chance of being desired. But if we accept ourself as we are, if we let our buried, repressed desires come out, then everything is possible.

Our partners can be decisive in helping us feel comfortable with our bodies and our sexual feelings. At all costs, we cannot allow ourselves to be controlled by repressive and narrow views unwilling or unable to accept the force and intensity of this vital drive which society would have us hide, snuff out, or channel into other areas.

If the prevailing morality, suddenly so prudish where we are concerned, tries to ignore or sweep under the rug the existence of sex even between married couples who are growing older, it does not take much to imagine the scorn and mockery heaped on those whose relations fall outside the norm. How can women with less traditional sex lives escape suffering and shame when they know—or believe—that fingers are being pointed at them, that they are being tarnished with lewd terms such as "dirty old lady," "nymphomaniac," "whore," or "aging dyke" when they pursue relations that are necessary for them?

Some years ago a curious story about a male prostitute appeared in a French women's magazine. He talked about his clientele, who in the absence of love or other possibilities paid for a little relief for their hungers, and about what they were implicitly seeking beyond the purchase of his "services." This young man, who sells himself to men as well as women but who specializes in women over forty-five, confided: "They are far more affectionate than the men. They don't see me solely as a means of satisfying their physical needs—they have a great need for tenderness. Often, my clients are unhappy in life. They are alone, terribly alone."

Very different from these women of secret and "unacceptable" pleasures are those who cling pathetically to love as to an elixir of youth. It is a way of denying their age, and one senses that they are less attached to their lovers or even to love itself than to the badge of youth they supposedly confer.

Finally, there are women who, despite society's prohibitions on their age group, view sexuality as a sign of vitality connecting them to themself and those they love, but who nonetheless see their libido decline or become blocked. Not wanting to lose this precious gift, they are anxious and unhappy about the defection of desire, and want to find the cause so as to remedy it.

It is clearly not easy for us women to be liberated with ourselves, our feelings, and our bodies in a social environment that rejects such freedom and seeks to make us conform to its own ideas on how we should be. There is virtually no place where we do not encounter that oppression whereby women over fifty are judged not according to their own lights, but according to a standard reflecting the traditional male preference for young and beautiful women—fresh, slim, round in the right places.

Two fundamental questions arise. First, are all men's desires formed by the pinup? Are there none who may be susceptible to the sensuality, the eroticism of a body where life and the years have left their traces? Are there none with a taste for the kind of relationship—marked by humor, complicity, a certain freedom and spontaneity of word and gesture—that is more possible with older women?

The second question, which is at the heart of this book, is: Why do women allow themselves to be dismissed from active life? Why do they not even put up a fight, when their hopes and desires, their bodies, their entire way of being are denied, refused, ridiculed? They set themselves up for defeat and then complain and are bitter about it.

We have to get to the bottom of why we have internalized and adopted these norms, making them the rules and justifications of our behavior, however much they make us suffer. In some ways we have been the accomplices of this premature "retirement" from the stage. Do we not use our body with contempt or negligence, ignoring its rhythms and demands, when we allow ourself to slip into a sexual sleep before our time? We all know women who look upon themselves, sexual beings that they are, with the kind of scorn that the sixteenth-century French· poet Clement Marot expressed when he repelled an unwanted woman:

> Dost thou wish to hear, with thy old wrinkles,
> Why I cannot love thee?

The same physical characteristics of face and body that are put in a flattering light for men are cast in ridiculous and cruel terms for women. A "noble and distinguished" face in a man of fifty becomes "puffy" in a woman the same age. Wrinkles in a man denote seriousness and wisdom; in a woman they recall an old hag.

The negative effect of this way of looking at things is well illustrated by a patient who complained of losing her sexual appetite when her breasts began to sag. "My bust was my only good feature," she said. The feeling of distance she developed toward her body because of the undue importance given to this "part object" (her breasts) distanced her as well from the body of her husband, who ironically did not share her repugnance.

Our entire experience and observation of life show us that even those who are ugly, ordinary, or faded are loved just the same. Deep emotional ties are formed because of other qualities we have—our vitality, our gifts, our intelligence, our heart, our instincts, an indefinable something. If the body has its place in all this, it is not because of its strict adherence to the standards of physical perfection or its eternal youth.

When we were young, in fact, how was it for us? If we were pretty, did we always know it? How did we use whatever beauty we had? We were prepared to lead boys on, then to refuse them, if possible, according to the rules of that rather perverse little game called virginity. In our chaste romances of adolescence, we were sometimes flattered but embarrassed by the desire the young men fixed on our timid bodies, which we perhaps saw as of secondary importance. Their impatient desire became a bit irritating or disappointing if we did not feel ourselves admired for reasons other than our physical charms. Now that those youthful charms are gone, is it possible that we have totally reversed our priorities? Is it now our hope that men, instead of recognizing us for what we are, will continue as long as possible to see us primarily as sex objects, even if we do not intend to give in to just anyone?

We are also consciously or subconsciously affected by the absence of love. Even when we no longer dare to love or let ourselves be loved physically or even know we miss it, life is there, waiting. Unable to express itself freely in sexuality, it can convert itself into distress.

The yearning for an absent, lost love can also express itself clearly, directly, and with the full force of its sadness. Hélène Cixous, the highly acclaimed French feminist author, writes: "Everything is lost? Everything. Except the desire to kiss, to remember an embrace, to taste again this lost mouth. Or rather this desire for love to enfold you once again. To remind you that what has been, was. Is no longer. The anguishing taste of never again, with an energy that's enough to make the dead sigh." For many women, this throbbing frustration can quicken their desire, emphasize their solitude, stir up their imagination, and keep their libido on tenterhooks, casting about for an available object: the first man who comes along. Otherwise, what to do with these useless but still functioning drives, sometimes even heightened at menopause by sudden influxes of hormones?

When a woman feels she can expect nothing more from her spouse, because of lack of understanding, boredom, contempt, physical disinterest, or neglect, one solution is to seek substitute "objects" to fulfill her various desires. She may well love her husband, but suddenly she feels the weight of time, the pull of a "last fling" before "retirement," the wish to taste those unknown pleasures that have been paraded unceasingly under her nose for the past thirty years by the mass media. How irresistible they can seem, these last-chance adventures! And sometimes fate intervenes to lend a hand.

The "last chance" can take many forms. There are more or less conventional love affairs. But popular morality is not kind to a woman who strays, particularly if she is not young. No one knows this better than women, but it can be tempting to flaunt your successes when you feel you are being hustled into an early retirement.

Certain women sleep with the first opportunity, though without much conviction, to get back at their husband for his infidelities, to make him jealous, to prove to him that they are still attractive, or, more crudely, to give the one who scorns them a kick in the teeth. In such instances, the weapon may be new but the kind of interaction was established long ago.

There are also those who seek passing solutions, one-night stands as it were, sometimes with money changing hands. In other words, the solution used by many men—their brothers in misery in this case—except that men have all the means at their disposal for satisfying themselves. For women, it is far more difficult if not impossible, and undoubtedly very disappointing, followed by the inevitable return to their solitude.

There are those who are attractive to young men for the simple reason that they are no longer young. In sometimes rich and tender affairs, they can free the young men of their Oedipal fixations and act as a transition between the mother and a partner their own age. Unfortunately for these women, such relationships with rare exceptions are ephemeral and leave them devastated, their heart in shreds, and their sexual energy drained.

Other women turn toward solutions without even realizing their true aims and objectives. They undertake psychoanalysis, for example, finding there a convenient and available man. It does not matter that sex is not part of the picture: they come to expect of the therapist what they want and often cannot obtain from their husband: attention and understanding.

When partners of the opposite sex are unavailable, or when they are threatening because of their demands or off-putting because of their selfishness, there is another possibility: homosexuality. One investigator reports: "Many women who were heterosexual up to mid-life subsequently turn to homosexuality. Is it because inhibitions and taboos are disappearing? Or because women, by predisposition as well as by tradition, are more indulgent concerning the 'esthetics' of their partner? . . . Some newly homosexual women told me that they were pushed by the selfishness of a partner who had aged as much as they, but who were repelled by signs of aging on them, toward a partner who did not treat them as an object, but as a being."* In fact, it is very often more a question of complicity, mutual support, and homosensuality than of outright sexual exchanges.

Changing one's orientation is not easy. Those who take a female lover or companion must often give up many other relationships, such is the hostility to this form of love.

Finally, there is masturbation, that dreaded word among yesterday's adolescents. Today, it remains a last resort for those who are alone.

Short of actual sexual encounters, working women sometimes express regret at the gradual change in attitude of their male colleagues, with whom relations previously were characterized by a more or less erotic undercurrent. There are no longer implicit ad-

*Dominique Desanti, *La Nef* 63 (Paris, 1977).

vances to accept or reject, no longer an appreciative or even frankly lusty twinkle in the eye, no more suggestive remarks. Much of this we could do without, of course. But aside from outright harassment or the kinds of abuse to which young women especially are sometimes subjected, many women do appreciate the harmless interest conveyed in words and glances, the small attentions—sometimes neglected by their spouses—which boost their self-confidence. Why deny that for many of us this kind of bantering or human warmth is one of the pleasures of our professional life, even if it does make our husband jealous and offend our feminist sensibilities? Thus, when men's eyes upon us begin to shift into an asexual neutrality, we may take this as a blow to our identity as a woman. The Simon Report on French sexual behavior found that women over fifty who work are more active sexually— the report does not specify with whom—than those who do not. We may speculate that the reason is to reaffirm their femininity and cancel out this devaluation of their sex.

But such an explanation covers only one aspect of why working women maintain their vitality. Work is itself a stimulant, maintaining one's interest level and a healthy competitiveness. Work is struggle, effort, a necessary human interaction. It forces one to maintain one's dignity in front of others on a daily basis—in dress, moods, behavior—with or without the wish to be seductive. It indirectly feeds the libido.

We can allow ourselves to be so strongly influenced by the fear of what others see that we exaggerate our wrinkles and physical shortcomings, which may in fact be less noticeable to others than to ourselves—like the dust under the sofa that is only visible to the mistress of the house. On the other hand, pessimism, bad humor, and spitefulness are far more disfiguring than the marks of time and kill any attraction one might otherwise feel toward us.

We are very often more loved than we think, especially since at this stage in our lives we are close to and needed by an entire affective network. The gratification arising from these ties is generally not sexual or even sensual, but there is an undoubted narcissistic satisfaction—not always easily recognizable since relationships of love and friendship thrive more on support and tacit complicity than on declarations of feelings. Could that be what we are missing?

Whatever the state of our sexual desires in the post-menopause (generally after the age of fifty-five), the body can, in the absence of appropriate treatment, lose its effectiveness as a vehicle for pleasure. Increasingly sagging or flabby breasts are not helpful in promoting erotic sensations or images. Far more important is the fact that the vagina becomes progressively thin and dry due to the diminution of hormones, and can become painful during intercourse, leading to frigidity and avoidance of sex.

These problems can be treated medically, as we shall see in a later chapter. The real danger is giving up, allowing ourselves to sink into the kind of self-disgust that prevents us from seeking treatment. The battle should be waged on two fronts: combatting the unhappy physical realities while exploring positive evolution in the realm of love and desire. Like good wine, they can take on a new richness with age.

There is obviously neither a precise date nor a general rule concerning these changes or withdrawals in one's love life. Many women remain sexually active well into old age. If this is not widely known or recognized by the public, it is perhaps because happy couples don't advertise themselves or don't make news. Then, too, "mature" women are not given the floor to speak openly and encourage other women who dare not believe in or strive for such activity. Men remain silent on the issue, too, seeing no cause for glory in ties or liaisons with women who are, to say the least, well past thirty. It hardly matters that we may have acquired not only a tenderness but also an eroticism lacking in younger women.

If partners the same age want to retain a physical taste for each other despite the fatigue of years, they must have regular sexual contacts. At their own rhythm, certainly—forget the so-called norms! Statistics are sometimes most off-putting. What is beyond question is that erotic stimulation attentively maintained is as important for the vitality and longevity of desire as the regular drawing off of water from a well is necessary to keep the source flowing.

At this stage in our life, when we may be insecure about this aging but not yet old body of ours, we have a special need for the renewed, indulgent, tender, and encouraging attention of our partner. He can find in us new chords—there is no body of whatever age that does not retain some curve or corner of innocence.

For many couples the same age who previously had difficulty synchronizing their pleasure, this can be a time to share the progression of erotic play. With the man's desire concluding less quickly in orgasm, the couple can enjoy the same cadence, slower and more subtle. Rather than taking the change of pace as a foretaste of impending defeat, they can give themselves over to the pleasure of unhurried, leisurely caresses. The pleasures of sharing, of reminiscing, of private jokes. When things don't work out, they can take it lightly, with humor, and wait for the next time.

Later, when the emotional and sexual life of a woman or a couple has exhausted a certain range of exchanges, others can be discovered. Simone de Beauvoir distinguishes between two sources of pleasure: one linked to one's own physical beauty, which decreases with age, and the other related to emotional desire and a corporal tenderness which is independent of age.

As the partners grow older, this "corporal tenderness" can assume an increasingly important dimension in their love life. The primacy of genitality can gradually give way to other approaches. This does not imply a regression of the relationship, since an entire past inhabits the present. Rather, it is a transformation, a refinement of certain perceptions which in the past were perhaps masked by haste and passion.

Sexual desire in women rarely disappears entirely. In later years, it finds other pleasures and satisfactions through a diffuse sensuality above and beyond orgasm itself. A woman's body is capable of remaining susceptible to a tenderness which is by no means an expedient to mask frustration.

What is to be hoped is that these possibilities and gifts do not remain dormant, unknown, or experienced in solitude. May each of us, at our age, find a salutory middle ground between unhappy extremes—between night and the body's silence, on the one hand, and a self-imposed sexual frenzy, complete with morose simulated pleasures and pornographic gadgets, on the other.

Orgasmic power, in either man or woman, is not the only criterion of personal value nor the be-all and end-all of human happiness. Those who are misguided on this point—who push themselves beyond the limits of their health, imagination, and seductive powers in order to worship at the altar of sexuality as the one true religion of human relations—will be sadly disappointed as age descends upon them.

Sexual activity is both the source and the highest expression of the vital energy we hope to keep for a very long time. But we must not become its slave. Beyond the bright flames of Eros, our emotional life will follow its course, with its joys and sorrows, its pleasures and disappointments, until we draw our last breath. Life goes on, even if, as has been said, the body of passion shrinks to the measure of melancholy.

What will we retain of the long history of our emotional life, of our experience of love? What will stay with us? Doubtless—and primarily—the fact that love and sex are not worn out from the using, despite what we were told as young girls so that we would "save ourselves" for our husbands. We have generally noted that, under different forms and toward different poles, the tendency to love can multiply the capacity to love. There are among us women who have been broken by personal dramas in love and cannot subscribe to these lines. But how many others have been able to gather into their hearts husbands, parents, friends, children, and even lovers, without any of these complementary loves ever being diminished because of the others? Love does not divide into portions, and tenderness only grows with more tenderness. Unfortunately, women are often the only ones who know that no one is wronged, and they are forced to juggle themselves, sometimes wrenchingly, among the jealousies of those they love.

We have undoubtedly learned and accepted by this time that young love's burning desire for oneness—for fusion with the other—is unrealizable, that there exists in the encounter with friendship or love a threshold that cannot be crossed. "The other is closed off," the psychoanalyst Jacques Lacan has written, forever beyond the reach of desire, even at the very moment our thirst is being partially and provisionally quenched, even when we are most together, even in the most totally reciprocal love. How capable are we today of accepting this inevitable and necessary distance, this relative or profound solitude even in the warmth of another's embrace?

It is starting from our clear-sightedness and tolerance in relation to this basic question that we can live the evolutions of love without being wounded, accept what is missing, and enjoy what is offered to the fullest. This realization can help us change our behavior. It can enable us not always to respond to the demands of our partners and not feel guilty about it. It can also help us moderate our own demands on them, leaving between us some space, a margin of freedom necessary to both.

Once we survey the extent and boundaries of the realm of love—rich, vast, sometimes dangerous—we must not, when faced with difficulties, use them to justify a bitter retreat into our egocentrism. Let us not be more fearful today than we were yesterday. We must not doubt ourselves. We still can maintain our taste for risk, tempered by wisdom, and set out again each morning to meet the lover, even if we never truly reach him. For along this stretch of road it is possible to come together, however fleetingly, however threatening this may be, and it is this that makes the journey endlessly recommenced worth while.

We know this today.

We should perhaps add to this general overview a few words about the sometimes crushing extra burden placed on many women by their working conditions and social class.

When working-class women reach fifty, they often have behind them a vast accumulation of years at manual labor—some of them have worked ever since their teens. Their jobs remain hard and repetitive today; the factories and shops in which they work are often uncomfortable or unhealthy. We have seen women in spinning mills carting enormous bales of cotton that add up to several tons a day, knowing they will have to do so day in and day out until they retire.

Many of these women have had numerous pregnancies, and sometimes miscarriages or necessary abortions, which took a heavy toll on their bodies. This, along with a low-cost starchy diet often eaten on the run, leaves few chances for keeping their figure. Too fat or too thin, they can only laugh at the notion of keeping up with the fashions; indeed, they must make prodigious efforts even to maintain an interest in their appearance and health.

Their salaries are low, which diminishes them in their own eyes; it also spares them any temptation of "impulse buying" or being unduly influenced by advertising—they can hardly afford the bare necessities. What self-image can they possibly have when constantly confronted on television or at the movies with the "ideal" model of the stunning, well-dressed sophisticate or perky middle-class housewife?

What rights do they grant themselves and what economic possibilities do they have to alleviate the physical effects of aging? Health spas, cosmetic surgery, a good hairdresser, thermal baths, smart clothes? Even attractive eyeglasses or dental work may be beyond their means.

Office workers, too, have spent their entire working lives ruled by the constraints of their jobs—repetitive and compartmentalized work, impatient or abusive bosses. The employers are often young men who take advantage of their dedication, and at their age they must still submit to the constraints of hierarchy as if they were youngsters.

Many of them live in the suburbs of big cities and have long periods of commuting each day. Their legs and backs show the effects of too much sitting and too much standing. The work, most often profoundly tedious, lets their minds lie fallow. Yet at group sessions, where they can express themselves freely, their aptitude for deep reflection and personal growth is clear.

Finally, they have to put up with the bad temper and derision of their younger colleagues if they complain or if they have different ways of looking at things: as already noted, there is little solidarity among women in the office setting.

Neither social struggles nor women's liberation have yet abolished the differences in opportunity that exist among women. What could, perhaps, bring us a bit closer together is the realization that in the last analysis, whatever our social background and class, we always remain to a greater or lesser extent the subjects of a society that measures our usefulness exclusively by our reproductive function.

· P A R T 2 ·

Prospects and Projects

IN THE FIRST part of this book, we confront a number of facts. What many of us had felt to be diffuse, indefinable, individual, or unfamiliar phenomena have taken on form and reality. Society is not kind to women our age and does not really know what we are.

Real changes are taking place within us, which many of us suffer from but do not understand. This book is based on the premise that our age can be put to our advantage. More often than not, it gives us the courage to look things squarely in the face, and this clear-sightedness is the first step to taking our lives in hand. Thus, however disagreeable the inventory we have been taking may be in places, there is nothing negative about it. We are by no means throwing in the towel, either for ourselves or for other women.

The difficulties of age are more obvious than its advantages. But the advantages are there, and they become striking once we focus not only on present fact but also on possibilities. We see that, among young children, cultural conditioning based on gender is being revolutionized, and the gap between boys and girls is being dramatically narrowed. Why should women our age not be particularly ripe for similar changes?

We have been liberated from our childrearing responsibilities and are less taken in by career games. We are often freer, stronger, smarter about life in general. We are more in tune with what is good for us: the medicines to take or avoid, the effects of coffee or alcohol on our sleep, how anxiety can manifest itself psychosomatically, how much we should weigh and the extra pounds that make us uncomfortable. We also know how to spot our pitfalls—the situations or partners that bring out the worst in us—and what to do to avoid them or overcome them.

Maturity has taught us—often to the benefit of others—the value of listening, of nuances, respect, and interest in what is different or unexpected. Our need for renewal (experience, after all, is our ever-decreasing ability to be astonished) pushes us to yet greater curiosity, invention, and discernment.

We are far from finished. We know how to work, to make love, to laugh, to cry, to dream, to listen—not to mention all our practical skills and talents—and often better than before. Perhaps we have also learned not to be taken in, either by soothing ideologies or fast-talking salesmen.

But why even bother to enumerate the qualities that age has given us or accentuated, and on which our spouses, children, parents, bosses, and others have come to rely? Don't they? Training and practice have made us extremely "reliable," and we are generally well aware of the extent to which we can count on ourselves.

There is a dialectical movement possible between weak points and strengths once we have a clear awareness of both and of how we can use them. In order to take advantage of the good things as often and as long as we can, we have to watch over three areas: our physical well-being, our psychological well-being, and—what derives from the first two—our social health, the ability to feel good with others.

· CHAPTER 8 ·

Physical Well-being

PSYCHOLOGICAL AND PHYSICAL well-being are so closely intertwined that the familiar expression "to feel good in one's skin" covers both at the same time. Our physical well-being becomes all the more important at this age, in that it can no longer be taken for granted: it is often less a question of maintaining good health than of getting it back.

There are several basic areas that deserve special attention, since they take on a primordial importance for women over fifty. One is the beneficial effects of fresh air and exercise, which keep us from getting sluggish, improve our breathing capacity, and help us lose the extra pounds we have been dragging around. Another is sleep, that precious but sometimes maddeningly elusive time of restoration. Then there is food, with its temptations, pitfalls, and pleasures.

• AIR AND EXERCISE •

If, as all too often happens, our body should become a source of misery and displeasure, at least let it be due to illness or some deterioration beyond our control, and not to our own negligence or ignorance about the human body's most elementary needs. Two of these are air and exercise: the least polluted air possible and exercise in keeping with the physical capacities we were born with and the present state of our heart and lungs.

A fifty-year-old woman is generally still in good physical shape, whatever discomforts of menopause, such as fatigue and hot flashes, she may be experiencing at the moment. Her heart and back should still be sound, even if she has not been exercising, and she should still have a good lung capacity. Naturally, if there has been abuse of alcohol or tobacco, the lungs and heart will show the effects.

In the absence of unhealthy addictions, hereditary or congenital illness, or defects resulting from childhood illness, adult ailments, or surgery, a large number of women over fifty are robust, full of energy and stamina, and capable of strenuous efforts. Many, unfortunately, do not believe in their own capacities or have acquired bad nutritional and overall health habits.

Most of us do not get enough fresh air and exercise. Through negligence or lack of time, we have allowed our muscles to become soft, especially the back muscles. We thus have to put up with frequent backaches, which are exacerbated by poor seating posture at work, pent-up emotions, badly resolved conflicts, and all the things we repress and which settle into our body. For many of us, the neck is fragile and painful. The muscles of our chest are poorly developed and so contracted that we do not know how to breathe deeply. Our feet are so badly muscled that they have become flat, squeezed into shoes that deform in the name of some ill-conceived notion of elegance.

Our skin, on the other hand, is frequently in good shape, the cosmetics industry having so ensnared us with their advertising that almost all of us eventually get around to buying a whole array of night creams, day creams, moisturizing creams, and revitalizing creams.

In the pressures of our life as wife and mother, many of us developed bad habits simply because we could not find the time to devote to our own health. There were always children to be driven somewhere, the baby that needed changing, our husband's requests to be attended to, dinner to be made, errands to be run. But there were other reasons as well, buried deeply in our personality, inculcated in us since childhood by the female social role we are called upon to fulfill: we are far more concerned with our external appearance, with being well made up and groomed, than we are with the long-term benefits to be derived from engaging in sports, spending as much time out of doors as possible, or walking places instead of driving or being driven.

When the French actress Madeleine Renaud, already well past fifty, was asked the secret of her youthful appearance, she replied simply: "A few exercises every day." How many women can afford *not* to perform the stretching and relaxation exercises that are indispensable to treating lumbago, chronic back problems, stiff neck, or migraines? It is not a question of shirking our responsibilities to home and family, but we cannot carry them out effectively by being compulsive or neurotic about them. Why not respect our bodies as much as our furniture?

There are women who have managed to set aside time to exercise. Many more could develop the habit, and it is for these women that we have selected a few simple movements requiring only a few minutes a day.

Some women balk at the restrictive and somewhat codified nature of the various exercise programs and prefer either walking or other outdoor activities such as swimming, strenuous gardening with its bending and kneeling, chopping and stacking firewood, cycling, camping, and so on. The problem here is that the exercise is intermittent and not sustained, subjecting our muscles and heart to an infrequent but perhaps overly vigorous workout. Nonetheless, these women are more likely to go out wholeheartedly for activities they enjoy than for some steadier, more regular exertion, and they should not be discouraged.

Those who are naturally athletic generally continue to practice their favorite sport, even noncompetitively. Jogging, currently very much in vogue, has its enthusiasts in our age group, but we should go about it gradually, after consulting a doctor, and at our own speed: there is nothing that requires us to keep up with our teenage son.

Certain changes in our routine to help us get more exercise are easy to make. We can break certain lazy habits, such as using the elevator instead of the stairs. Climbing up a few flights clears the lungs, helps circulation, and builds the leg muscles. The same can be said for walking. If we have to go a mile or so, our legs will carry us far better than the bus or car. And how should we spend our weekends, aside from the usual household chores? Going to the movies or walking in the woods? Spending the day knitting and watching television, or taking the grandchildren or friends to the swimming pool?

Working out, exercise, and vigorous activity are not the entire story in staying fit and taking care of our physical well-being. We should also be able to pamper ourselves for an hour or two at least once a week without feeling guilty about it, spending time in a leisurely hot bath, followed by creams and powders, doing our nails, our legs, and other tasks whose most important function here is relaxation. The simple act of massaging ourself under the shower, for example, running our hands over our body, recognizing it, kneading it without critical hostility but simply to feel that it exists, *as it is,* can give a completely natural pleasure and help keep us in tune with what is good and necessary for our physical self. Women in sleek advertisements for soaps and bubble baths are not the only ones who have the right to linger over their bodies. We all need to break the frenzied pace of our everyday life and to fall whenever possible into a slow, deep rhythm, where our gestures are more deliberate or left to intuition and the precision that only leisure can allow them.

Painting, sewing, embroidering, bookbinding, gardening—any hobbies or labors of love—are all, in their fashion, sources of the body's well-being. Another is time spent with our small grandchildren, reading to them or telling stories, playing with them, sharing with them. These are among the blessings of nature that we crave in our rushed and urban lives.

Our bodies also need to breathe in fresh air, to enjoy the sweet smell of the sea, of new leaves, of freshly turned soil. They need landscapes and wide horizons that do not burn or tire the eyes. They need silence. Sometimes they need to learn the taste for a certain solitude: getting in touch with our own breathing and being able to go where we like, to eat or sleep when we like, to listen to our own cadence, at least for once, before going back to the tempo of others.

The few exercises that follow are the fruit of thirty years' experience observing women. Selected from dozens of others, they are a condensation of what a rheumatologist, gynecologist, sex therapist, and physiotherapist might recommend. (They should not be confused with yoga positions, which are extremely useful as well but which require a teacher's guidance to be effective.) Their objectives are to maintain our overall health and fitness, improve our general circulation and flexibility, and help us keep a younger silhouette by improving our posture: the spinal column should be as close to a straight vertical as possible when we are in a standing position (see figure 5).

At rest, we normally breathe in sixteen times a minute and take in about a pint of air. In deep-breathing exercises, we can take in up to a quart of air in a single breath (do not repeat this kind of breathing too quickly, or dizziness and other problems may ensue).

Before starting, take stock of your usual posture and see what distortions need correcting. Look at yourself in a full-length mirror in the nude, both full face and in profile. When standing, your spinal column should be as close to a straight vertical as possible. Pay special attention to the position of the head, whether it is tilted forward or not; whether or not the back is rounded or arched; and whether or not the stomach and buttocks are pulled in. The goal is to eliminate the curves and the compression of the spinal column brought about by muscular neglect, and to try to recover the vertical of your figure.

EXERCISE 1

This exercise is aimed at improving the breathing.

Spread a mat on the floor and get a small cushion to put under your neck (this can also be used for sleeping if you have neck pain).

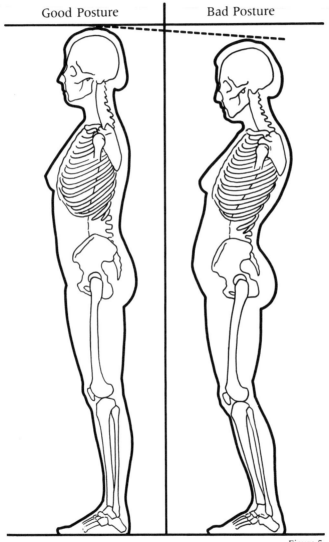

Good Posture   Bad Posture

Figure 5

Position

Lie down on the mat.

Stretch out the spinal column, trying to draw it out from the top of your head as if someone were pulling you by the hair.

Press your shoulders flat against the floor.

Spread your legs so your feet are about twelve inches apart and make sure your back touches the floor at all points (check with your hand).

Raise your knees and keep your feet and back flat on the floor.

Breathing

Inhale deeply, letting the stomach expand as you do (it doesn't matter if the back raises a bit from the floor during the inhalation).

Exhale slowly, expelling all the air from your lungs, pulling in the stomach and flattening the back against the floor as you do.

This exercise should be repeated five or six times in a row, at the rate of about three per minute.

EXERCISE 2

Position

Stand with your back against the wall, your feet about six inches from the wall and slightly spread, your knees slightly bent.

Press the *entire* spinal column against the wall, the small of your back pushed slightly outward, the pelvis slightly tilted (see below). The head as well as the shoulders should be pushed down and back, and the entire back must be tight up against the wall.

Extension

When exhaling, pull up from the top of your head (as if you were trying to appear taller).

Use your hand to make sure you are still in the right position, with your back completely touching the wall at all points, from the neck to the buttocks.

Relax and inhale deeply.

This exercise should last from thirty seconds to one minute. Do three or four in a row, if possible both morning and evening.

Pelvic tilt

Remain standing and gradually straighten your head, with your chin drawn in, so that it is directly aligned over your back. Look straight ahead toward an imaginary horizon.

Push your shoulders down and back.

Pull in your stomach, tighten your buttocks, and contract your thigh muscles.

These movements, when well coordinated, tilt your pelvis to make you stand straighter and prevent you from arching the back too much, which curves your upper back and makes your stomach stick out. Exhale while performing the tilt.

This good posture also increases your lung capacity. It not only restores the spinal column to its full length but releases the roots of the sciatic and lumbar motor nerves, as well as those of the sympathetic and parasympathetic nerves.

Make sure that holding a good posture does not prevent you from breathing normally (pulling in the stomach while inhaling, letting it out while exhaling).

EXERCISE 3

The following movements are designed to improve mobility of the head and flexibility of the neck. They improve the circulation in the brain and thus ward off the dizziness connected with cervical arthrosis.

Position

Sit on the mat, your back straight, neck stretched straight up, knees bent with your hands clasped around them, feet flat on the floor and slightly apart. (You can also sit cross-legged, which is a good position for the perineum; see exercise 6.)

Pull your shoulders down and back.

Movements

(Stop at the slightest pain.)

Slowly rotate your head on the axis of the neck, making the

widest circle possible while facing straight ahead. Repeat several times in a row, first in one direction, then in the other. Do not force.

Turn your head as far as possible three times over your left shoulder, three times over your right, three times with your chin pointing toward the ceiling, and three times with your chin touching your chest. (For this movement and the one following, when looking over your shoulders keep your gaze horizontal; you can choose a point at the edge of the field of vision on each side.)

Drop your head forward, your chin touching your chest. Let your head fall to the left, then back, then to the right, making the widest possible circle with the chin. After two or three circles in one direction, repeat in the other. (For this movement, relax the jaw; it is normal for it to open slightly when the head is thrown back.)

EXERCISE 4

Position

Lie down on the floor and raise your legs straight up, keeping your knees straight.

Press your back flat on the floor and stretch out your neck, keeping your chin down.

Keep your arms at your side or your hands clasped behind your neck.

Movements

Make *horizontal* scissors movements with your legs. The width of the movements should be about ten to twelve inches.

Make the same movements *vertically.*

Spread your legs and snap them tightly together repeatedly in quick movements.

Alternate all these movements.

For all these exercises, exhale slowly during the movements and inhale during the rest periods.

EXERCISE 5

Position

Lie down with knees bent and feet flat on the floor and slightly apart, as in exercise 1.

Keep your back flat against the floor and your arms at your side.

Movements

While *exhaling,* raise your shoulders and the upper part of your torso and look at your belly button.

Lie back, relax (breathe in and out), and repeat.

EXERCISE 6

Position

Sit cross-legged or on a chair.

Keep your back straight, your arms at your side.

Movements

Make circles with your shoulders, keeping your arms relaxed.

Breathe in when you raise your shoulders, breathe out when they fall.

Feel your shoulder blades rub against your back.

Do not do more than four or five shoulder circles a minute.

When you begin these exercises, particularly if you have reached middle age without doing any kind of workouts, you can expect to have to overcome a great deal of stiffness. With each passing week, you will gradually increase your flexibility and extend your stretching movements, giving a real sense of accomplishment. We have seen many women over sixty, stiff-jointed and totally out of shape, get into the habit of these exercises to such an extent that they could no longer do without the pleasure of their morning "uncoiling."

Finally, we want to call attention to the Kegel exercise, also called the "elevator," which was developed by the American obstetrician who first noted the importance for women of the muscles of

the perineum. It can be performed at any moment of the day and can turn wasted time, such as that riding buses or subways or waiting in line at the supermarket, into time well spent.

The perineal muscles, which support the uterus, vagina, ovaries, and bladder and which also carry the weight of the intestinal mass, are too often ignored by women who do not even know they exist. In fact, they play an important role in our sex life, as well as in pregnancy and childbirth. We can become aware of these muscles and tone them simply by tightening the anal sphincter muscles, which simultaneously tightens the vagina. The movement is accentuated by tightening the abdomen and buttocks.

Contracting the perineal muscles improves the circulation of the lower pelvis, which sometimes cures stomach cramps arising from a reduced flow of blood in the veins. Training these muscles can also stave off prolapsed or weakened bladder, which often troubles women over fifty. An added benefit: these muscles, once trained, can heighten the intensity of pleasure during the sex act.

If you simply cannot seem to get into the habit of exercising regularly on your own, as a last resort it would be worth your while to ask your doctor to prescribe fifteen or twenty sessions of massage and physiotherapy of the sort designed for circulatory problems or pain in the back and ligaments. The physiotherapist will help you get into training.

· S L E E P ·

Many women begin to have sleep-related problems around fifty. Those who always had trouble sleeping have even more trouble now, and a great many of those who always slept well begin to experience the deterioration of this precious gift that enabled them to recuperate from whatever discomforts and worries the day brought.

Is there anyone who does not fear insomnia? It is a rare person who knows how to adapt to it or manage it. Night accentuates the anguish of solitude, physical ills, and even hostility. How much mental energy is wasted waging battles that prove futile with daybreak! Then, too, there is the simple worry that the following day we will not be in shape to carry out our responsibilities.

Insomnia is a well-known member of that procession of ills linked to menopause or middle age. One cause is often the hot flashes that can awaken us in the middle of the night, followed or not by profuse sweating. Above and beyond the purely physical discomforts that disrupt our sleep, there are feelings of insecurity and strangeness, the sense of having become different. If insomnia comes in the early hours of dawn, we are unlikely to be able to get back to sleep, unless it's just before the alarm goes off!

At fifty, all too often real emotional, social, and health difficulties undermine our nervous system and threaten to disrupt the sleep so indispensable to our well-being. Sometimes the difficulty of realizing ourselves as human beings can cause insomnia, compounding the perturbation in the hypothalamus. In certain cases, insomnia can be due to illness whose psychosomatic origin does not make it less real. This sickness can engender anxiety and anguish, and lead to depression.

Depression exists at all ages, but it is more marked at menopause. Its primary manifestations can be physical, simulating stomach or heart ailments, causing dizzy spells, debilitating fatigue, and headaches. Or the nervous or mental aspects can predominate, in which case lack of interest, indifference, and loss of enthusiasm for life and one's loved ones are more pronounced than the physical symptoms. With depression comes insomnia, which in turn aggravates the depression in a vicious circle. How to break the cycle? The depression will have to be treated before hormone therapy is undertaken, or at least at the same time.

Antidepressants are one of the great medical discoveries of our era. We should not hesitate to use them, especially since they in no way interfere with other means of combating insomnia, such as massage, yoga, shiatsu (a kind of pressure-point massage) and acupuncture, which has scored real successes in the treatment of sleeplessness. Nor do they prevent us from seeking professional counseling to help work out our problems.

Barbiturates, on the other hand, must be avoided at all costs.

While giving a deceptively restful sleep, they in fact upset the architecture and structure of truly beneficial sleep by suppressing the REM phase (during which dreams occur) so necessary to the health of our nervous system. In certain specific cases, and under medical supervision, tranquilizers can be resorted to, but this really must be the exception and the doses and duration must be prescribed by the doctor. But the doctor is not in our shoes, and it is up to us to determine the *minimum* dose that is effective for our system and then to try to do without it as soon as possible. We have to be on guard not to let these medications become narcotics.

One of the casualties of our fast-paced, nervous lives, so in thrall to the exigencies of the modern world, is contact with the personal, instinctive, basic rhythm that characterizes each one of us. And yet, like all living things, whether plant or animal, we do have a rhythm that follows the alternating ebb and flow of energy.

Obviously, we know that there is day and night, winter, summer, autumn, and spring, and that these changes influence our behavior and way of life. We know about the moon's influence on certain biological events and on moods. We know the influence of the seasons on certain viral or bacterial diseases, or on triggering asthma or heart attacks.

What is less known is that we have personal rhythms in the alternation between sleep and wakefulness, throughout the day and night. Science has progressed in the knowledge of these biological rhythms through studying sleep patterns.

The story of research into human sleep is an exciting one. It was previously believed that there were only two kinds of sleep: the light sleep of sleep onset and dozing, and the deep sleep that followed. Sleep was believed to be a passive act—one let oneself drift off to sleep. Sleep was a kind of annihilation likened to death by poets and writers. In mythology, Morpheus, god of dreams and sleep, gathered into his arms the sleeper, inert and abandoned, fit only to be visited by dreams heavy with prophetic or mysterious import.

The work of the past twenty years reveals that sleep is on the contrary a constructive act, complex, varied, infinitely structured and positive—the very antithesis of passivity. It is an activity that is absolutely indispensable for our physical, mental, nervous, and even moral and philosophical health.

Sleep can be compared to a carefully constructed building; if it is disturbed, its architectural structure is altered. Such disruptions have many causes. One is the deterioration of our physical equilibrium because of an infectious or metabolic illness (the level of potassium, calcium, magnesium, urea, sugar, or acidity in the blood) or because of a neuro-endocrine imbalance, as at menopause. A disturbance in the balance of our emotional life, such as personal or family worries, can also cause our sleep to deteriorate, which in turn adversely affects our physical health in a classic psychosomatic syndrome.

We can utilize the new knowledge about human sleep and the successive stages within a given sleep period for our own personal ends. The five stages of each sleep cycle are discussed below, and are summarized in the table that follows. There are three to five complete sleep cyles, each with five stages, per night.

After having found the most comfortable sleeping position (rituals differ from person to person, and even for the same person vary with age), we enter the sleep-onset stage, which lasts from five to fifteen minutes. Whereas in a waking state our brain waves register from eight to twelve cycles per second on the electroencephalogram (EEG)—the rhythm called "alpha-wave activity"—during this phase of falling asleep the EEG tracing is four to six cycles per second. Hence the name *slow sleep.*

Then comes *light sleep,* which lasts from ten to forty minutes, with an ultra-slow rhythm on the EEG accompanied by slow breathing.

The next stage is *moderate sleep,* lasting ten to thirty minutes, with a drop in blood pressure and body temperature and even slower EEG tracings (two to three cycles per second).

Deep sleep follows, a state of profound relaxation offering maximum rest and recuperation. This stage lasts ten to twenty minutes.

These first four stages are also called NREM (non-rapid eye movement) sleep, to distinguish them from the fifth and final stage in the sleep cycle.

A NORMAL SLEEP CYCLE
(3 to 5 cycles each night)

PHASE	DURATION	EEG	REACTIONS
Sleep onset	5–15 mins.	Stage I: slows to 4–6 cycles per second	Physical relaxation, diverse mental images
Light sleep	10–40 mins.	Stage II: some shallow cycles	Reveries, breathing pauses
Moderate sleep	10 30 mins.	Stage III: slow waves	Drop in temperature and blood pressure
Deep sleep	10–20 mins.	Stage IV: very slow waves	Profound muscle relaxation
REM or paradoxical sleep	15–20 mins.	Fast, weak cycles	Total muscle relaxation, rapid eye movement, intense dream activity

The final stage is called *REM* (rapid eye movement) *sleep*, so named for the intermittent bursts of rapid eye movements which characterize it. It is also called *paradoxical sleep* (PS), a term coined by the French scientist Michel Jouvet to emphasize the contrast in this stage between total muscle relaxation and intense cerebral electric activity, with its rapid cycles and high voltage, as well as the rapid eye movements.

The REM stage is the one in which dreams occur, and if we are awakened at this point we can generally remember, if only fleetingly, our dream. But being brutally wrenched from a dream is a shock to our nerves and very unpleasant for our psyche. Unfortunately, the demands of our timetable or our married life do not always take into account the progress of this phase of our sleep.

Because of our dreams, this stage of our sleep is absolutely essential for our overall state of health. It is here that fatigue is swept away, that recollections are sorted out, information processed—in short, that memory stocks are created. Our ego and personality, as well as our ability to make plans and carry them out, are evidently all strengthened during this period.

It should thus be clear how essential it is, after fifty, to sleep well and to dream well. The physiological disturbances at menopause that affect the hypothalamus and all the nerve centers which cooperate to produce a sound sleep are natural, and we are advised not to interfere with nature. But allowing nature to become a "bad mother" and interfere with our sleep handicaps our present and our future, our memory, our vital force, and our will to make the most of our life.

There are good and bad sleepers, but they are not always who they think they are. Waking up four or five times a night does not necessarily mean we sleep badly; there is nothing wrong with awakening for a few seconds between sleep cycles and dropping off to sleep again. The very belief that we sleep badly, however erroneous at the outset, can become a self-fulfilling prophecy, and sleep can actually deteriorate because of the misconception.

On the other hand, there are those who believe themselves to be sound sleepers because they sleep straight through the night but who wake up tired, spent, a little nauseated, discouraged. Upon looking into the causes, sometimes it turns out that barbiturates are being used to prolong what was perhaps a natural sleep period of five hours but which the person feared to be inadequate. As already mentioned, barbiturates reduce the quality of sleep by acting on both the NREM stages and the paradoxical stage, disrupting or suppressing dreams. They also create a dangerous addiction and can sometimes even become a stimulant.

Hormone treatment can help us regain a sound sleep, with estrogen acting as a natural antidepressant and progesterone as a natural sedative. As already mentioned, when absolutely necessary we can also supplement the treatment with certain artificial antidepressants and tranquilizers, in small doses and for short durations, although it is better to do without them.

Many women are pleasantly surprised by how quickly hormone therapy acts upon the nervous system. Women who have been insomniacs for some time become sound sleepers once again (or for the first time), able to fall asleep within ten or fifteen minutes and to wake up feeling pleasantly rested, up to the day ahead.

We should not expect miracles. Those who have gone all their lives needing only six hours of sleep, for example, will not suddenly require nine, ten, or eleven hours. Every individual has his or her own physical and psychological makeup, his or her own sleep needs—a hypnogram, as it were. We have to accept that. There is no point in wanting to change one's deeper nature or true personality.

Sleeping and dreaming are two complementary functions, and both are absolutely central to our well-being. During slow sleep, our muscles, heart, and respiratory system rest. In dream or paradoxical sleep, on the other hand, the brain recovers its balance: memory, adaptation to circumstances, attention, concentration, mental capacity, plans, creativity.

Even if we think we do not dream (only five percent of people report dreaming) because we do not remember our dreams afterward, they perform a function that is essential to our psychic equilibrium. They are an unconscious defense mechanism serving to reduce the tensions that accumulate and are more or less repressed during the day. They escape our control; we are not responsible for the images they bring. They can be charged with emotion, complex, seemingly incoherent, even indecent, humorous, beautiful, or repellent. Our entire psychological life and the people who play a role in it appear in these images, which express our feelings and our otherwise unacceptable or impossible desires. For the most part, the events and people depicted are in disguised form, for our dreams, like our entire unconscious life, are subjected to our moral censorship.

It is important not to dramatize the messages that dreams bring us: we must learn to come to terms with our ambivalence. As human beings, we are neither all angel nor all beast in our unfulfilled desires, but perhaps a little of both. If we are unduly troubled or curious about our dreams, we can always talk about them to counselors or psychologists who can help us understand or accept the past or present repression they betray. They may even help us dare to try to realize some of these unfulfilled wishes.

Aside from medicines, there are a thousand and one little "tricks" for recovering the sound sleep so necessary to us. These can be very useful to people with occasional bouts of insomnia, which, though not serious, produce great anxiety.

We all know from experience the enervating effects of coffee, tea, or alcohol. Going to bed too soon after a large, rich meal troubles our sleep. With age or fatigue, we are less able to tolerate the effects of alcohol, and a congenial dinner with friends can result in nightmares or a sleepless night.

Impatiently awaiting sleep never fails to drive it away. If we pass the sleep-onset stage without being able to fall asleep, there is no point in getting upset about it. We might as well utilize the time needed to fall asleep (about forty minutes) agreeably or usefully. Why not make a silent tour of the house, take some air, read a bit, put some order in our papers? We can also use insomnia more creatively, putting an overcharged brain to work developing some good ideas, making plans, or simply reflecting on our life, and our good fortune to be alive.

Some practical details: a high-quality bed, sufficiently wide and firm, is not a superfluous luxury. Nor are well-designed lighting units that give each partner in a double bed a certain autonomy. These small improvements may not be enough for couples who sleep very lightly and end up ruining each other's moods and lives by thrashing about. In such cases, it may be preferable—without making too much over it—to have separate beds or even separate rooms if possible. This can avoid the wearing of nerves that compounds the wear and tear of age.

Finally, if by and large we sleep well, let us not exaggerate the minor sleep disturbances we sometimes have. An occasional sleepless night lets us see how lucky we are not to be real insomniacs, who, while we sink voluptuously into the sweet forgetfulness of an easily accessible sleep, are left to await the dawn counting sheep.

• NUTRITION AND DIET •

Whether or not we feel guilty, in our Western nations of abundance, at the thought of the millions suffering from hunger, we are all, as we grow older, more or less affected by illnesses deriving from a very real overnutrition. At the same time, we women are haunted by an obsessive fear of obesity, sometimes real but very often imaginary. Far from "living to eat," we grant ourselves—and with increasing stinginess—the right merely to "eat in order to live." We know that historic, psychological, and sociological conditioning combine to make our figures a primarily esthetic issue, even if we pay lip service to health and comfort (especially moral comfort—the comfort of conforming through our efforts as closely as possible to the "ideal" body).

For many women who rightly or wrongly fear being overweight, the problem may lie in struggles and influences dating back to their childhood. As little girls, they were expected to be pretty and neat, but were subjected to eating habits that did not always promote this end. They bowed to others' expectations of them with varying degrees of submission or opposition, depending on the quality of their relations with their mother and the value of the advice their mother gave them.

Such advice was often coolly rejected in adolescence, that turbulent period when we vacillated between the desire to please and the despair of ever being pleasing to anyone. Thus arose a certain anarchy concerning food, with periods of fasting alternating with binges.

The less attractive adolescent girls consider themselves, the more they eat, thus entering a classic vicious circle that is difficult to break. Some women revert to the same behavior at menopause, and for the same reasons—even if they have passed the age of acute conflicts with their mother. The more anxiety-ridden they are, the greater the consolation, distraction, or escape they will get from food. Alcohol, which also causes weight gain, often plays the same role.

If weight really is a problem, it is time to think about going on a diet. But a diet, in order to be followed, must take into account the would-be dieter's overall personal and family situation. To impose a draconian (a thousand calories a day) diet on someone who is always hungry and who has good reason to nibble and eat precisely what should not be eaten is to guarantee failure, pushing her to pathetic cheating, disappointment, and self-disgust that she will try to forget in—what else?—food.

The problem is thus first to treat the anxiety or the bad habits and then to undertake a diet, which should start off being easy, in order to give the dieter self-confidence and strengthen her resolve. It goes without saying that no one, and especially not the doctor, has the right to make an obese woman feel guilty through reproaches; obesity, like alcoholism, is an illness and should be treated as such. On the contrary, it is important for the doctor to provide encouragement.

Before starting a diet, find out how much you weigh, and weigh yourself every few days if you are not satisfied.

If you do decide to go on a diet, try to analyze for *whom* (or because of whom) you want to lose weight: your husband, your children, your parents (an obese mother or father can make you terrified, sometimes irrationally, of an extra five pounds). Analyze *why* you want to lose weight: is it for health reasons, to feel more comfortable, to be able to dress better, to look better in the mirror?

Learn the composition of the principal food groups. There are three categories of energy nutrients: proteins to build up muscle and body tissue; carbohydrates to burn energy and to work; and fats or lipids for energy.

Inform yourself about the difference between saturated fats (mainly animal fats, such as butter and lard) which are bad for you, and unsaturated fats (mainly vegetable, such as sunflower-seed oil, wheat-germ oil, etcetera) which are not. Look into the importance of animal and vegetable proteins, where they are found, and how to use them.

Among the foods you like, learn which are bad for you and try to develop a distaste for them, or resist them by cutting your appetite. To cut your appetite before meals, drink a large glass of water, eat half a slice of bran bread, or swallow a tablespoon of gelatin with a bit of water. Concentrate on your wish not to gain weight, on the pleasure of getting back into clothes you have outgrown or recovering your old figure. If necessary, lie down for five minutes to regroup your willpower.

To cut your appetite between meals, drink a glass of water at least every few hours. Do not let yourself get too hungry. If you are very hungry, drink a glass of skim mik or eat a cup of plain low-fat yoghurt, raw vegetables such as celery or carrots, or unseasoned vegetables cooked in advance, such as green beans, tomatoes, eggplant, or zucchini. If you are really starving, you can eat a slice of cold lean meat.

Always eat at least three meals a day. Skipping meals is a sure way to become so hungry that at the next meal you eat more calories than you are capable of burning, which means the surplus will be stored as fat. Use salt sparingly, and replace sugar by artificial sweeteners. Better yet, cut out sweeteners entirely and learn to appreciate the true flavor of tea or coffee. Begin to rely on seasonings other than salt and mustard, such as thyme, parsley, onion, garlic, tarragon, chives, lemon juice, and so on.

Eat lean meat in moderate amounts, either broiled or roasted rather than fried, and whenever possible substitute fish and poultry (with the skin removed) for red meats.

Do not fall into the trap of thinking that butter alone is fattening—oils are equally so. When you must use oil, use sunflower, wheatgerm, corn, or soy-bean oil, which contain unsaturated fats less dangerous than animal fats for the heart and arteries. And do not replace butter with unlimited amounts of margarine; it is, after all, a fat and cannot be used with impunity.

If you are afraid of nutritional deficiencies while dieting (and strict diets should never be followed for long periods except under medical supervision), do not hesitate to take multivitamin supplements containing one RDA (Recommended Daily Allowance) for vitamins and minerals.

Above all, don't be obsessive about your eating habits. From time to time, allow yourself a "forbidden" treat.

Below are two samples of reducing menus, recommended by the Bureau of Nutrition of the New York City Department of Health, one at 1,200 calories a day and the other at 1,600 calories a day. (In the West, we generally consume about 3,000 calories a day, whereas a person leading a sedentary life needs only about 2,000 to maintain the same weight.

PORTION SIZES

FRUITS (no added sugar)
High vitamin C:
$\frac{1}{2}$ small cantaloupe, $\frac{1}{2}$ grapefruit, mango or papaya
1 medium orange or tangerine, $\frac{3}{4}$ cup strawberries
4 oz. orange, 5 oz. grapefruit, or 8 oz. tomato juice

Others:
1 small apple, pear, or banana
1 medium peach or nectarine
2 medium apricots or plums
2 tbsp. raisins
$\frac{1}{2}$ cup grapes, cherries, blueberries, raspberries, blackberries, or
  pineapple
$\frac{1}{8}$ medium honeydew melon
1 cup watermelon
$\frac{1}{2}$ pomegranate
$\frac{1}{3}$ cup pineapple or apple juice
$\frac{1}{4}$ cup grape or prune juice

PROTEINS
(Limit red meats to 16 oz. a week and no more than 4 eggs per week)
1 oz. poultry, lean meat, fish, or canned tuna or salmon
1 oz. part skimmed hard cheese
2 oz. cottage, pot, or ricotta cheese or queso blanco
3 sardines or 5 clams, shrimp, or oysters
1 medium egg
$\frac{1}{2}$ cup cooked legumes (reduce bread by 1 portion when using
  legumes)
$1\frac{1}{2}$ tbsp. peanut butter or 3 oz. tofu

BREADS
1 slice bread
$\frac{1}{2}$ bagel
$\frac{1}{2}$ pita bread
$\frac{1}{2}$ English muffin

$\frac{1}{2}$ matzoh
2 graham squares
6 thin crackers
4″ pancake
5″ waffle
6″ tortilla
$\frac{1}{8}$ slice of 14″ pizza

GRAIN PRODUCTS
$\frac{1}{2}$ cup cooked cereal
$\frac{3}{4}$ cup most ready-to eat cereals (not presweetened)
$\frac{1}{2}$ cup cooked rice, all pastas, buckwheat, bulgur wheat, grits
$2\frac{1}{2}$ tbsp. flour

STARCHY VEGETABLES
$\frac{1}{4}$ cup sweet potato
$\frac{1}{3}$ cup corn
$\frac{1}{2}$ medium ear corn
$\frac{1}{2}$ cup potato, peas, or winter squash
$\frac{1}{2}$ cup cooked legumes
$\frac{2}{3}$ cup parsnip
$\frac{3}{4}$ cup pumpkin

MILK OR SUBSTITUTE
1 cup (8 oz.) skimmed milk, skimmed buttermilk, or plain low-
   fat yoghurt
$\frac{1}{2}$ cup evaporated skimmed milk
$\frac{1}{3}$ cup skimmed milk powder

VEGETABLES
($\frac{1}{2}$ cup cooked or 1 cup raw)
High Vitamin A:
Broccoli,* carrots, dark green leafy vegetables (beet, collard,
   dandelion, mustard, and turnip greens, escarole, kale,
   parsley), red peppers,* Swiss chard, watercress, pumpkin,
   winter squash

*Also good sources of vitamin C.

Others:

Asparagus, bean sprouts, beets, bok choy, Brussels sprouts, cabbage,* cauliflower,* celery, cucumber, eggplant, green beans, green pepper,* lettuce, mushrooms, onions, summer squash, rhubarb, sauerkraut, tomatoes

Potato or Substitute:

$\frac{1}{2}$ cup potato, peas, or winter squash

$\frac{1}{2}$ cup cooked legumes (lentils, chickpeas, lima beans, soybeans, etcetera)

$\frac{1}{2}$ cup cooked rice, all pastas, grits, buckwheat, or bulgur wheat

$\frac{1}{2}$ cup plantain, yautia, or dasheen

$\frac{1}{3}$ cup corn or $\frac{1}{4}$ cup sweet potato or 1 slice bread

POLYUNSATURATED FATS

1 tsp. oil: safflower, corn, sunflower, soybean, or cottonseed (do not use palm and coconut oils)

1 tsp. margarine (first ingredient on the label should say liquid)

1 tsp. mayonnaise

2 tsp. salad dressing

6 small walnuts

MONOUNSATURATED FATS

1 tsp. olive or peanut oil

5 small olives

10 peanuts or almonds

2 large pecans

$\frac{1}{8}$ avocado

1,200 CALORIE MENU
(FOR MOST WOMEN)

Breakfast

High Vitamin C Fruit: one portion
Protein Food: one portion
Bread or Grain Product: one portion
Milk or Substitute: one portion

Lunch

Protein Food: two portions
Bread, Grains, or Starchy Vegetables: two portions
Vegetables: two portions raw and/or cooked (not Potato or
  Substitute)
Fruit: one portion
Milk or Substitute: one-half portion

Dinner

Protein Food: three portions
Raw and Cooked Vegetables:
  a. High Vitamin A: one portion
  b. Other Vegetables: eat freely from those groups labeled High
  Vitamin A and Others (except beets, carrots, onions, pumpkin,
  or winter squash; limit these to $\frac{1}{2}$ cup)
  c. Potato or Substitute: one portion
Fruit: one portion
Milk or Substitute: one-half portion

Snack

Fruit: one portion

Fats

Three portions daily

1,600 CALORIE MENU
(FOR LARGE-FRAME WOMEN)

Breakfast

High Vitamin C Fruit: one portion
Protein Food: one portion
Bread or Grain Product: two portions
Milk or Substitute: one portion

Lunch

Protein Food: two portions
Bread, Grains, or Starchy Vegetables: two portions
Vegetables: two portions raw and/or cooked (not Potato or
    Substitute)
Fruit: one portion
Milk or Substitute: one-half portion

Dinner

Protein Food: four portions
Raw and Cooked Vegetables:
    a. High Vitamin A: one portion
    b. Other Vegetables: eat freely from those groups labeled High
       Vitamin A and Others (except beets, carrots, onions, pumpkin,
       or winter squash; limit these to $\frac{1}{2}$ cup)
    c. Potato or Substitute: one portion
Bread, Grains, or Starchy Vegetables: one portion
Fruit: one portion
Milk or Substitute: one-half portion

Snack

Fruit: one portion

Fats

Four portions daily

   Doctors and nutritionists who deal with weight problems are
unanimous in warning against the dangers of refined sugar in
every form—whole or in soft drinks, desserts, ice cream, and so on.
The reason is that each time sugar enters the bloodstream, the
blood glucose level rises suddenly and the pancreas secretes a hormone called insulin which helps store calories in the form of fat.
Furthermore, insulin removes sugar from the blood very quickly,

so the glucose level drops and the sensation of hunger returns. The sugars (or simple carbohydrates) are thus bad for three reasons: they bring large amounts of calories for a small volume of food; they are burned very quickly, calming hunger only briefly; and they encourage the formation of fat deposits.

Complex, slowly assimilated carbohydrates (such as those found in natural grains, rice, pastas, and vegetables), on the other hand, do not trigger sharp increases in the glucose level and consequently do not have the same drawbacks as the simple carbohydrates. Bread, which is a complex carbohydrate, can be eaten in moderation or eliminated from the diet entirely as need be. If you are very hungry or become constipated, there is no harm in having a slice of whole-grain bread or bran bread (less fattening but not always well tolerated) with every meal.

There is, unfortunately, no substitute for the hard work of a carefully designed diet. Beware of the shortcuts or miracle formulas that are often advertised in magazines aimed at women, such as pills, reducing belts, and other gadgetry. These things are not necessarily harmful—they simply do not work and are costly, and those who use them (especially those who make financial sacrifices to buy them) can become so discouraged that they give up and do not try anything else.

On the other hand, some reducing methods can actually be dangerous, and we must be on the lookout for charlatans (even if they do have medical degrees) who recommend and prescribe them. Three groups of drugs, taken alone or in combination, must be avoided.

Appetite suppressants (or amphetamines) act on the nerve center for hunger in the hypothalamus. They give the sensation of being full, so you no longer feel hungry. But these drugs also act on the neighboring nerve centers and, after a short-lived euphoria, cause anxiety and an unhealthy stimulation. Such products are especially dangerous for the woman over fifty, whose main problem in this turbulent period of her life is to find a new equilibrium.

Diuretics are synthetic chemical products designed to stimulate to the point of irritation the kidney cells, which then eliminate salt through the urine, causing weight loss. But at the same time that the sodium is being eliminated, there is also a loss of mineral salts such as potassium, which are indispensable for the body's biological balance. It is not easy to make up for this loss of potassium through replacement potassium. Moreover, if large doses of diuretics are absorbed over a period of time, whatever weight loss there may be will be accompanied by exhaustion and heart problems. As soon as the diuretics are discontinued, the weight shoots back up, often beyond what it was in the first place. The price of this futile venture is often several million damaged kidney cells, a strain on the heart, and sometimes depression.

Particularly scandalous are falsely homeopathic pills combining appetite suppressants, tranquilizers to counteract their negative effects, chemical diuretics, and, as a last straw, thyroid extracts.

Thyroid extracts deserve special treatment. They are indeed extremely useful in the case of hypothyroidism, when the thyroid gland has slowed down and is no longer functioning at its normal level. This sometimes occurs at menopause, at the same time the ovaries cease to function.

Among the symptoms of hypothyroidism are the tendency to feel cold and shivery, a puffy face, dry and brittle hair, split or striated nails, weight gain, and increased cholesterol levels. Only a doctor, after thorough and meticulous examination, can prescribe the necessary dose of thyroid extracts.

If the thyroid gland is functioning normally, thyroid extracts must be avoided at all costs. Any weight loss they cause is in the wrong places: the muscles lose their tone and become soft, while the fat deposits are little affected.

The dangers of these three types of medications are illustrated by a 1977 court case in France, where three doctors "specializing in weight reduction" were found guilty in the death of a twenty-one-year-old woman who had followed their prescriptions to the letter.

The subject of weight clearly must trigger a considerable amount of anguish for women to put their health, and even their life, in the hands of strangers supposed to be magicians. There must also be considerable ignorance concerning the fundamental rules of nutrition and the functioning of the human body. Like human sexuality, facts about nutrition and health should be taught in the schools from the earliest age and not left to be gleaned haphazardly from gastronomy and advertising circles. It is unacceptable, and even scandalous, for so important an area to remain the province of doctors and specialists.

What dark broodings we attach to our image of the ideal body, and especially to our image of our own body! It is not unusual for women who are in fact normal to become obsessed by what they see as an extra three to five pounds, to the point that they discontinue their hormone treatment on the grounds that it causes weight gain. In fact, this is not so, at least not generally, any more than the birth-control pill causes weight gain. Moreover, the doses administered in hormone therapy are lower than in the regular contraceptive pill. On the other hand, since hormone therapy improves the health and the overall equilibrium, it can improve the appetite, which makes it absolutely necessary to know what a proper and balanced diet consists of and to stick to it.

There is a considerable range of "ideal" weights given in charts put out by various sources. The New York City Department of Health recommends guidelines put out by the Metropolitan Life Insurance Company for women between the ages of twenty-five and fifty-nine. They appear below. Women our age should generally go by the higher numbers. Unfortunately, women—particularly those over fifty—are haunted by an entire sociocultural conditioning against "plumpness" or "having a little meat on the bones." The "ideal" weights sometimes recommended are more appropriate for fashion models: 120 pounds for 5'7", 110 pounds for 5'5". From a medical standpoint, these are aberrations which impose on their victims the discomfort of being continually hungry.

HEIGHT	SMALL FRAME	MEDIUM FRAME	LARGE FRAME
4'10"	102–111	109–121	118–131
4'11"	103–113	111–123	120–134
5'0"	104–115	113–126	122–137
5'1"	106–118	115–129	125–140
5'2"	108–121	118–132	128–143
5'3"	111–124	121–135	131–147
5'4"	114–127	124–138	134–151
5'5"	117–130	127–141	137–155
5'6"	120–133	130–144	140–158
5'7"	123–136	133–147	143–163
5'8"	126–139	136–150	146–167
5'9"	129–142	139–153	149–170
5'10"	132–145	142–156	152–173
5'11"	135–148	145–159	155–176
6'0"	138–151	148–162	158–179

Weight in pounds in indoor clothing weighing 3 pounds and shoes with 1 inch heels.

It is true that extra pounds put undue pressure on the heart and bones and make everything more difficult—walking, any physical effort, work, the choice of clothes, and so on. But what constitutes "extra pounds"? There is a different answer for each woman, according to her physique, metabolism, and heredity. If a woman was always stocky, or if her parents and grandparents were heavy or obese, her "ideal" weight will not be the same as for the woman who was always average or on the thin side and who suddenly, within the past few years, puts on twenty pounds. We cannot speak of an absolute, ideal weight, only of a weight that is appropriate for this or that particular woman, one that suits *her,* enabling her to dress in a way she finds pleasing, to move comfortably, to come to the dinner table and eat her fill without anxiety.

When there is a real weight problem, a diet should be undertaken. But which diet? Once again, there is no single diet, but diets adapted to each individual case. The appropriate diet should be developed by the doctor, on the basis of a thorough physical examination and laboratory analyses (blood and urine tests, etcetera), and the woman herself, in keeping with her own possibilities in terms of time, lifestyle, and willpower.

Our weight is partly a question of heredity, but it also depends on age. To keep our sense of proportion, it is useful to bear in mind that women of normal weight frequently gain gradually over the years, so that by the time they reach fifty they weigh about ten percent more than they did at twenty-five. Each woman is, of course, free to want to keep the same weight she had as a youth, but it will soon be apparent that this requires more discipline: we generally use fewer calories at fifty than we did at twenty-five and burn them more slowly and less thoroughly. In order to maintain our same weight, we have to eat less while using more physical and mental energy (intellectual activity also burns calories, the brain being a large consumer of glucose).

There are numerous methods of weight reduction which are described in detail in scores of specialized books, and your doctor or public health service can usually give you a safe diet. For our purposes here, it is enough to say simply that a basic knowledge of nutrition and diets is essential (and not very difficult to acquire), and everyone should work out her own food plan with the help of someone with expertise in the area, such as a doctor she trusts.

To control the extra bulges here and there and the skirts that feel tight after the holiday season, there is nothing like cutting out alcohol, white bread, and high-fat foods for a while (not to mention sugar, presumably already eliminated from the diet). The only thing usually missing is the courage to do so.

• HORMONE THERAPY: BENEFITS AND LIMITATIONS •

Although lifelong habits of good health and a good fighting spirit are unquestionably our best allies in weathering the storms brought by menopause, there is no reason to disdain the undeniable help offered by hormone therapy. But hormone therapy is a long-term treatment, involving a certain number of decisions and choices.

As we know, the ovaries stop working around the age of fifty.

For the few years prior to that, there are only traces of progesterone in the system. With menopause, there is very little estrogen, in quantities varying from one woman to the next.

In the first months and even the first years of menopause, there are temporary variations in estrogen levels which cannot be predicted with any regularity: sudden increases, then decreases, then resumption, and finally a falling off to near zero. It is the extreme reduction of estrogen that causes the unpleasant symptoms of menopause: hot flashes, night sweats, the loss of vaginal lubrication, and the whole array of physical discomforts that take place around fifty.

Until a few years ago, estrogen alone was prescribed to eliminate these symptoms and compensate for the hormone loss. It subsequently became clear that this was a mistake, and today progesterone is always prescribed in conjunction with estrogen. The two hormones are complementary and synergistic; together, they act harmoniously, reinforcing each other while preventing the ill-effects that one of them alone could cause.

Estrogens stimulate the blood vessels, accelerating the circulation. When carefully controlled, this improves the blood supply to the tissues. When excessive, it causes edema through a leakage of blood plasma into the connective tissue. Edema in the breasts causes swelling which can sometimes become painful. Edema can also occur in the waist area, causing abdominal swelling, and in the ankles.

Estrogens also speed up cell growth and result in a proliferation of new cells. When excessive, this can produce an overly rapid growth of tissue, which is called hyperplasia. If it occurs in the lining of the uterus (the endometrium), it can cause hemorrhaging. In the breasts, it can cause cysts or encourage the growth of tumors, benign or malignant.

None of these problems, caused when estrogen is administered alone, occurs when the two hormones are taken together. Indeed, progesterone regulates, moderates, and tempers the action of estrogen while not reducing its advantages. In a way, it acts as an anti-estrogen hormone; that is, if the body had manufactured too much estrogen or we had received it as a drug, the progesterone would intervene to offset and neutralize it. And when there is a strong contraindication to taking estrogen, progesterone alone can give good results. (Progesterone is also administered alone when hormone analyses show that sufficient estrogen is still being produced.)

The physical and psychological benefits that result from hormone treatment are considerable. Estrogen acts as an antidepressant, restores or maintains muscle and nerve tone, and gradually eliminates apathy and fatigue. Joy of life and enthusiasm for things and one's loved ones return. (But if there is an overdose, estrogen can cause nervousness, aggressivity, and instability.) Progesterone acts as a tranquilizer, but without the unpleasant side-effects. It restores our equilibrium and eliminates aggressivity and irritability.

Naturally, life's circumstances do not change. There are no miracles. Women who live under difficult and unfavorable socio-economic conditions will continue to struggle, but at least they will now have the weapons they had lost for the last few years. Many women report recovering their sense of balance and feeling that they have reintegrated their personality, from which they had felt detached at menopause.

Two to three months after beginning the therapy, one's former capacity for work returns. After six months to a year, there is an overall sense of well-being. We do not have the physical capacities of a thirty-year-old, we do not become new again, but we can enjoy life with a body that responds.

The journey toward aging differs from one individual to the next. We have genes for longevity which make us more or less capable of resisting its effects. But within these limits, we have a real margin of personal maneuver. Our actions can make a difference, and one of those actions is recourse to hormones.

To sum up, hormones combat fatigue and improve sleep. They allow better blood circulation to the cerebral, nerve, muscular, dermal, epidermal, and mucous cells. For example, skin and muscles age less quickly, and mucous membranes remain supple and resistant.

They indisputably have an antisclerotic and anti-arteriosclerotic effect. The mechanism, though not well understood, has been documented by clinicians.

They improve the flexibility of the joints. Very often this is accompanied by a disappearance of aches and pains in the joints (in all likelihood due to improved blood circulation in the joints and surrounding ligaments).

They prevent thinning of the bones and further loss of calcium. Depending on the person, this effect on the bone mass can be either preventive or curative, particularly in relation to osteoporosis, a metabolic illness of the bone characterized by a progressive loss of the skeletal mass. Osteoporosis evolves silently and insidiously over the years before becoming serious, painful, and sometimes crippling. It is much more common in women than in men and it accounts for the loss of height due to softening and flattening of the vertebral bones and for the so-called "dowager's hump."

The connection between osteoporosis and the loss of estrogen was first discovered in 1940. It is a fact that bone pain largely disappears in women suffering from osteoporosis when they are treated with hormones. Other hormones (such as calcitonin, a parathyroid hormone) are also involved in laying down calcium in the bone and, with the expected advances in medical research, in coming years we will undoubtedly be able to determine how bone loss is due to deficiencies in the ovarian hormones and how much to deficiencies in other hormones. Whatever the case, our present state of knowledge makes it reasonable to rely on hormones to improve the condition of bones and ligaments after menopause.

With hormone treatment, the face takes on a more relaxed appearance because of hydration of the skin (the epidermal cells are no longer dried out and renew themselves) and a firming of facial muscles (due to a reactivation of elastic fibers). Although the transformation is neither radical nor miraculous, the unquestionable hydrating and tonic effect constitutes the kind of improvement that can encourage us to undertake the steps described elsewhere in these pages—an exercise program, a balanced diet, and better health habits.

Without hormone treatment, fatty tissue predominates over mammary tissue in the breasts of practically all women over fifty.

With treatment, the process is stopped and even reversed. The breasts regain firmness, tone, and consistency which will be all the more striking if the hormone action is accompanied by exercises to develop the pectoral muscles and support the breasts.

Hormones cannot be prescribed if the doctor, based on a careful medical history and meticulous physical examination, finds medium or severe hypertension, serious liver impairment, circulatory disorders, disturbing biological signs indicating high blood-fat levels or diabetes, or extensive fibroids, endometriosis, or mastitis.

Another contraindication to hormone therapy is a suspected family predisposition to breast cancer (a mother, sister, or aunt diagnosed with the disease). A tendency to overweight could also make a doctor hesitate to prescribe the treatment.

But above and beyond these, what risks, if any, does hormone therapy involve? Frequently articulated concerns center on two issues: the risk of cancer of the breast or uterus, both organs high in estrogen receptors; and the risk of vascular accidents, embolism, and high blood pressure.

Fears within the medical profession concerning hormone therapy can usually be traced to very old experiments carried out on mice and other laboratory animals forced to absorb large doses of estrogen, totally out of proportion to the quantities prescribed in treatment. We are familiar with the experiments of Dr. Otto Mühlbock. Although the mice he worked on did indeed develop breast cancer after absorbing estrogen, the mice used were a special strain, genetically predisposed to this type of cancer.

These results have nothing to do with the incidence of cancer in women. Unfortunately, breast cancers also occur spontaneously in women, without any hormone treatment. Breast cancer is the most common form of cancer in women, so it is hardly surprising if some women undergoing hormone therapy should contract it.

It is true that hormone treatment administered during the 1950's, which used estrogen alone (made from an extract of mares' urine), did slightly increase the rate of cancer of the endometrium. On the other hand, many authors now maintain that treatment combining progesterone with estrogens closely resembling the natural hormones not only does not increase the frequency of breast and endometrium cancer, but actually diminishes it. There are logical reasons for this: the treatment's antihyperplastic effect and early detection promoted by the close medical supervision the therapy requires.

The ideal is to begin treatment as soon as there is progesterone deficiency (also called luteal deficiency). This deficiency sometimes appears before the age of forty, sometimes around fifty, and most often in the mid-forties. There are a number of ways or combinations of ways to determine if this has actually begun and menopause is near. The treatment will be determined on the basis of a careful history (general and menstrual) and a physical examination. Initially, small or medium doses of the hormones should be prescribed, which can be revised depending on the reactions observed after a period of two to four months.

Hormone treatment is prescribed during several successive situations over the years. At the beginning of the climacteric, when the cycle becomes irregular, the addition of progesterone regularizes it. Likewise, when a period is skipped every few months, progesterone makes it come back. In the months following the natural cessation of menstruation, very small doses of combined estrogen and progesterone generally do not bring the periods back. But if the dose is increased, monthly bleeding (though not a true period) resumes.

Reactions to the resumption of monthly periods vary. Some women, whose periods were painful or experienced as bothersome constraints on their professional or private lives, are extremely distressed to see them return. The doctor should take this attitude into account and make every effort to prescribe a dose high enough to produce beneficial results but sufficiently low so as not to trigger bleeding. Other women, on the contrary, see menstruation as the symbol of health, well-being, and youth, and want to prolong their periods for four, five, or six years following menopause. These women must be made to understand that the doses must be adjusted in keeping with the needs of the organism, its reactions and tolerance level. If monthly bleeding returns as a byproduct, so much the better, but this cannot be a goal in itself.

In practice, the doctor sets the doses of estrogen and progesterone at the first consultation, basing them on the indications for which the hormones are being prescribed. Once the dose is fixed, three months are allowed to pass in order to gauge its appropriateness. If the hot flashes disappear, if sleep is improved while the patient begins to sense an overall well-being, and if the bleeding at the end of the monthly treatment is acceptable, then the initial dose was appropriate. If, on the contrary, the symptoms persist, the dose can be increased even while carefully ascertaining whether certain symptoms (insomnia, for example) may not be due to other factors, such as a difficult conjugal, social, or psychological situation. If the hot flashes have disappeared but the breasts are swollen or painful, or if the bleeding at the end of the monthly treatment is too heavy, then the initial dose may need to be adjusted.

So the treatment is adjusted after three or four months, and will subsequently be reevaluated every six months, to make sure the prescribed doses are suitable. An appropriate evaluation should include a physical examination as well as a periodic endometrial sampling.

Generally, the side-effects associated with estrogen replacement include: unscheduled bleeding, enlarged and tender breasts, nausea, swelling, weight gain, headaches, and mood changes. Side-effects associated with progesterone include: bleeding, breast tenderness, weight gain, and depression. Insufficient progesterone may result in endometrial hyperplasia, bleeding, and changes in the breasts.

In summary, when there is an imbalance between estrogen and progesterone, various combinations of symptoms can occur.

The duration of the treatment depends entirely on its objectives. If it was undertaken solely to eliminate the hot flashes, fatigue, and insomnia connected with the post-menopause, a treatment lasting from six months to a year could suffice. However, longer term treatment may be necessary for action on the tissues and organs affected by estrogen loss and for the treatment of osteoporosis. In such cases, treatment can be continued for ten to fifteen or even twenty years. Indeed, for the time being, in the absence of any findings to the contrary, hormonal treatment can theoretically be followed indefinitely. The coming years will enable us to better gauge its long-term consequences.

Each physician has his or her own preferences in prescribing hormone-replacement therapy, involving cycles of twenty-eight or thirty days. An attempt is made to simulate the woman's cycle during her fertile years. The length of the cycle matters little. What counts is leaving a free interval at the end of the monthly treatment for the artificial menstrual period. Estrogen is generally prescribed for day one through twenty-five of the cycle, and progesterone is prescribed for day fifteen through twenty-five of the cycle and for a minimum of ten days. The two treatments thus end the same day, leaving several days free of replacement therapy during which the artificial period will occur.

There are, as can be seen, a few practical drawbacks for the women who follow the therapy: they have to organize themselves, stick to a calendar, keep track of the treatment, and not forget to take the hormone pills. Time passes quickly, and women with a lot on their minds do not always find it easy to follow this small daily ritual without making mistakes.

Estradiol or estrogen creams have a few clear advantages from a medical standpoint: they bypass the liver and consequently tire it less, cause fewer gastrointestinal side-effects, and permit lower doses. These are applied directly to the skin of the abdomen.

Hormone treatment requires relatively frequent medical check-ups, and it is sometimes difficult to find the right balance between over- and undertreatment.

Finally, reluctance within the medical community, not yet to-tally won over to the new methods, can be disturbing. But we do not get something for nothing. It is up to us to inform ourselves thoroughly, weigh the pros and cons, and decide what price we are willing to pay for the benefits of the treatment.

• NONHORMONAL TREATMENTS OF MENOPAUSE •

We have already mentioned the drawbacks of the hormonal treatment of menopause: inadequate information on the part of some doctors, the need for a series of laboratory tests, the rigors of applying the treatment to the letter if it is to be beneficial. We also have called attention to the contraindications to its use: previous breast or endometrial cancer, thromboembolism, phlebitis, fibroids, and medium or severe diabetes. Other contraindications include—though the medical profession is not unanimous on these—medium hypertension and hyperlipidemias (high levels of cholesterol and triglycerides in the blood).

Each case must be evaluated individually. The existence of nonhormonal treatments also plays a part in the decision, especially since hormonal and nonhormonal treatments can be used successively or in combination.

Let us take as an example the frequent case of a woman who reaches menopause with a medium or large active fibroid tumor. If estrogens are used, there is the risk that the fibroid will increase in volume. For two or three years or even more, nonhormonal medication will have to be used. When the fibroid has diminished, when the patient is about fifty-five or fifty-six, small doses of estrogen can be prescribed, under close medical supervision, in order to prevent osteoporosis and atrophy of the vagina and vulva—conditions which are not addressed in nonhormonal treatments. In the event of a fibroma, progestins—also a hormone treatment—are particularly useful and should be borne in mind.

Nonhormonal treatments of menopause include sedatives of the cerebral cortex, such as phenobarbital in small doses. Tranquilizers and antidepressants are effective for reducing anxiety and even hot flashes. But they have unpleasant side-effects. (It is sometimes necessary to combine them, briefly and temporarily, with hormone treatment, which is not always fully effective immediately.)

Medications that act on the diencephalus (hypothalamus and neighboring regions) are often well tolerated but not always effective. Some of them can cause a sudden weight gain, soreness in the breasts, or even galactorrhea (a slight discharge of liquid from the nipple). Tests on these products continue.

Finally, we recommend all practices that soothe the cerebral cortex and, through it, the hypothalamus. These include sports, walking, dancing, yoga, and all forms of relaxation. Their action is complex, occurring through various peripheral mechanisms in the muscles and circulatory system as well as through the central, cerebral, and diencephalic (hypothalamus and neighboring regions) mechanisms. They can result in the same equilibrium as hormonal treatment, except that they have no effect on osteoporosis which so frequently strikes women over fifty. If they succeed in producing the sought-after results, these practices also have the advantage of sparing women the dependence on medication which is an inevitable part of hormone treatment.

Whether or not you follow a hormone-replacement therapy, your doctor will certainly prescribe regular checkups. Women between the ages of forty-five and sixty should have Pap smears, endocervical smears, and possibly even endometrial smears once a year to make certain there is no cancerous or precancerous tissue. Early detection carries with it a high chance of cure.

Regular breast examinations are also an important preventive measure. In addition to monthly self-examination, it may be useful to have periodic thermograms and sonograms of the breast which are both painless and without risk. These tests can detect infinitesimal anomalies at an extremely early stage, thus making possible more effective treatment.*

Once we have carefully taken all these precautions, we should relax and not be obsessed by the fear of illness. And we must remember that one's organs do not constitute an acceptable topic of social conversation.

---

*Mammograms, standard X-rays of the breast, can be done every two years without undue risk of radiation. Thermograms, which measure rises in temperature levels inside the breast (fast-growing tissue such as that of a tumor is hotter than normal tissue), can be repeated without risk since they involve no radiation, but they are far less accurate. Sonograms, produced by the echoes of ultrasound waves, have recently benefitted from technical advances that make them worth looking into. Like thermograms, they can be performed at no risk.

• C O S M E T I C   S U R G E R Y •

What makes women our age who have lived so many years with their faces and bodies "as they were" suddenly want to have them changed, repaired, remade? There are many things that could lead us to ponder the possibility, even if we do not go through with it.

Often, even before this fateful age, we may have been tempted to conform more closely to the prevailing fashion of face and figure before it was too late, at whatever cost (extremely high, in fact!)— incentives and encouragement in the media and beauty clinics were not lacking. (To do justice to the current women's magazines, however: when they speak of cosmetic surgery, it is generally without pushing it and with considerable caution.) Throughout the ages, women have been subjected to this type of pressure under various forms, and they have, as one observer noted, "by turns painted, twisted, bound, depilated, starved, stuffed, tattooed, mutilated, and crippled themselves in the name of beauty standards presumed to be timeless."

Today, the possibility of "repairing the irreparable outrage of the years" is all the more inviting in that available techniques appear to have acquired a hitherto unequaled perfection. "Artifice" is henceforth in the hands of science. What a reassuring development!

We can remain totally indifferent to or scarcely affected by these siren's songs; we can poke fun at them, rail against them, feel repelled by this new hold of the market over our bodies. But whatever our initial reaction, we owe it to ourselves to look seriously at the present state of cosmetic surgery, if not to be able to choose for ourselves without prejudice, then at least to understand those who opt in favor of it. Which of us hasn't amused herself in front of a mirror, pulling back the skin of the face just to see what it would be like if the furrows were suddenly swept away and we looked like we used to? Isn't it tempting to imagine that it could magically stay that way?

Only the very young and the very beautiful dare make fun of those who have their skin tightened and retightened. It is true that many young people today profess the notion that everyone has the right to be who he or she is without shame, whether tall or short, fat or thin, black or white, man or woman, ugly or beautiful. But however noble this principle of dignity, it is often more illusory than real for those who belong to the less desirable categories. Rare are those who are so sure of themselves as to be able serenely to resist the prevailing opinion or judgment. And aren't aging women among the undesirables?

Above and beyond these rather depressing observations, there can be numerous serious motives for wanting to undergo operations of rejuvenation or improvement. Our career may require us to look young and elegant: our job security can depend on our physique, and we do not always have the option at this stage to change careers. Or we may have physical flaws which were tolerable until age accentuated and aggravated them, making it hard for us to live with them. We may fear that a relationship with a much younger partner will be compromised by too glaring an age difference. We may want to break with a certain number of elements in our past, including our features, in order to set off toward a new orientation in life.

We can tell ourselves that we do not want the gap to widen further between what we are deep down inside and what we look like. We are not as old today as our grandmothers were at our age, so why should we look it, when we can call upon medicine, surgery, or any means at our disposal in order not to?

We women have a way of interacting with our mirror, often without lies, without flattery; it speaks to us, and we hear with increasing frequency unpleasant reflections. Women do not experience the slackening of their features the way men do. One often notes this difference during sensitivity-training sessions while working on the "relationship to the body." Group members of fifty and sixty years old are asked to look at themselves in an imaginary mirror (such as a blank sheet of paper) and describe what they see, especially the details of their face they like and which can give them confidence in their relations with others.

Most of the time, the men do not know how to describe themselves. They say they do not look at themselves, but still they seem to accept well enough what they think they are or have become. (Nonetheless, men make up a large minority of the clientele of cosmetic surgeons. Among these are undoubtedly men who see themselves on television or movie screens.)

Women, on the other hand, generally know themselves well and do not forgive themselves any blemish—they depreciate themselves willingly and sincerely. They have to be helped to recognize what others find likable and attractive in their face and expression.

As human beings, we need to respect and like ourselves. Our face and body cannot be repugnant to us, causing us feelings of shame or inferiority. But how often are we unfair to ourselves, exaggeratedly harsh or discouraged? Can plastic surgery correct such an insecurity? Can it reassure us?

We are victims of our need to show ourselves to our advantage, both with those we love and with the stranger whose path we cross. We feel we have to look good (beautiful?) or close to it, just as we have to look clean and decent. It's a question of social decorum! Whether we are pleased or annoyed about it, the fact remains. For all these reasons, legitimate or questionable, the advances in cosmetic surgery attract us, trap us, or—for some—offer a new lease on life.

Whatever our reasons for being interested in cosmetic surgery, the important thing is not to plunge into the adventure without careful thought and reflection—alone, with friends who have our interest at heart, and with serious specialists who have been recommended by competent persons (our doctor, a friend who already underwent an operation, etcetera). The authors have mixed feelings about these operations when they do not seem absolutely necessary. We are not completely against them, if only because as women we know from experience that it can be tempting to recover the body and face of our youth, when they were more harmonious. But we are hesitant, because an operation, whether undertaken for reasons of medical necessity or otherwise, is a serious matter.

All these reservations lead us to reflect on the various implications of the decision. We can question our rejection of what time and character have done to our face. What is the source of this degree of disgust or refusal of self? Is this attitude toward our physical appearance shared by those close to us? And if we really do not like ourselves anymore, is it likely that we will be more at ease in a "renovated" skin?

Our relations with ourselves can be fragile and touchy. Being no longer able to recognize ourselves, even in improved form, can unleash feelings of confusion and disarray. "Touch-up" operations—eyelids, eye pouches, and so on—are less risky than complete facelifts, which when they fail can completely change our facial expression or freeze it into an inscrutable mask.

Nor should we forget that the skin, even after a successful operation, eventually slackens, and the results can last only five years. To repeat the operation several times is hardly a satisfactory solution, because it stretches the features excessively and finally can no longer hold. Do we want to risk presenting a face that no longer exists, a frozen mask incapable of conveying shades of meaning? This is the risk of failed or repeated operations. What is the appeal of looking "good," but being neither natural nor oneself?

We should be clear, too, about our motives, and not undertake an operation in the hopes of holding on to a husband or a lover who is losing interest. It is a trap to think that surgery will bring him back.

For those who are determined to go through with the operation, convinced that an improved appearance is essential to their deepest well-being, a few obstacles remain to be overcome.

First of all, there is the cost. Cosmetic surgery remains by and large the prerogative of the rich. Before even envisaging the possibility of surgery, one must know that these operations are expensive and not covered by private medical insurance, to say nothing of Medicare.

There is also the choice of surgeon, which is particularly important in a field where one cannot take for granted the honesty and competence of the practitioners. It is a market of supply and demand, of what the traffic will bear (and for certain wealthy women, it bears a great deal). It is also a market where "cooperation" is not unknown between beauty institutes and surgeons of few scruples and not necessarily great skill. Thus, it is absolutely necessary for us to dare to ask questions, to discuss the price, and to get a guarantee of rigorous operating conditions. Some doctors, taking advantage of our insecurities, do not facilitate dialogue. In such cases, it is best to look for someone else.

It is also important to beware of flashy publicity, assembly-line outfits, and dazzling promises; serious medical professionals do not resort to these practices. Beware, too, of before-and-after photos, which are often faked. The only surgeon worthy of your confidence is the one who will straightforwardly discuss with you your hopes and expectations concerning the operation, and who tells you honestly and realistically what he believes he can achieve on the basis of how you look now.

From a medical standpoint, plastic surgery with general anesthesia involves the same risks and requires the same precautions as any other operation. You will thus have to have a complete physical examination beforehand.

You should also make certain you understand that, medically speaking, the absence of wrinkles, even while improving your morale and general outlook, will in no way reduce fatigue, weariness, or any of the other problems of aging and menopause. Nor will it deal with the problems of your personal life.

Having expressed all these reservations, we can say that there are indeed extremely competent cosmetic surgeons and that this type of operation has witnessed great strides over the past decade. The surgery is now virtually painless, the scars are less visible, the results are more natural-looking and last longer, and there are fewer risks and failures than before.

Some surgeons refuse to perform certain kinds of cosmetic surgery until the client has shown real efforts to get herself in shape beforehand, for instance by losing weight. Facelifts, for example, should be merely one aspect of a whole way of confronting life and seizing its opportunities. This is a far cry from passive abandonment to the magic act or a panic response to a supposed disaster.

The restrictions and warnings expressed in the preceding pages may seem dated in a few years, and cosmetic surgery may become completely safe, accessible, and ordinary, enabling large numbers of women to prolong their youthful appearance without risk, failure, or excessive cost and with the collective approval of their fellows.

The following table gives some general facts concerning the present state of several popular cosmetic operations. Many can now be performed on an in-and-out basis, where the patient enters the hospital in the morning and goes home the same evening. Scars may disappear over time, but no doctor can guarantee it.

OPERATION	NIGHTS IN HOSPITAL	TIME OFF WORK	SCARS
Facelift	0–1	1 week	Invisible
Nose	0–1	5 days	Invisible
Eyelids or eye pouches	0–1	4–5 days	Invisible
Ears	0–1	2–3 days	Hidden
Drooping breasts	0–1	5 days	Small
Breast enlargement	0–1	1 week	Hidden or small
Tummy tuck	1 week	3–4 weeks	Small
Buttocks	1 week	3–4 weeks	Small
Thighs	1 week	3–4 weeks	Small

Is there life without facelifts? Most of us would respond with a resounding "Of course!" even though some may have a tinge of regret. There are a thousand ways not to let oneself go; there are other "tricks" more within reach that can help us remain physically attractive.

Good health and humor can be far greater assets than a face that "looks ten years younger" stuck on a woman who is impossible to live with. There are excellent beauticians who are not out solely to sell as many beauty products as possible—they can also teach the art of skillfully applying makeup, help us find a flattering hair style, and devise a good treatment plan for our skin.

Finally, and most important, there is a vital minimum of self-acceptance that gives a certain serenity to any face, even if we have to make a few concessions to "imperfection." We have to pay homage to our body, which has sometimes been driven hard, which has worked, delivered children, known pleasure and pain—this old comrade in arms which deserves both our care and our indulgence.

·CHAPTER 9·

Social Well-being

· WORK ·

ONE OF THE greatest concerns of women over fifty is to avoid the solitude and prolonged inactivity they did not have to worry about when family commitments were at their peak. And that means maintaining or carving out a place for themselves in the larger society, beyond the couple or the immediate family. Without in any way minimizing the appeal of the family and the importance of family ties, they are no longer enough to give women our age (or today's younger women either, for that matter) the clear and lasting sense of being useful, respected, and capable of progressing. It is thus important to maintain or develop other connections—people from the outside world with whom to work, have fun, share interests, take classes, or engage in political activities—and to discover with them and through them another way of becoming oneself.

For a great many women, an active career will fill this function, at least in part for a few more years. Those who have been able to keep a place in the working world—even a modest one, even one based on tiring and repetitive tasks—should stop to think about what this activity means for them in terms of intellectual and physical stimulation and human contacts. Beyond the obvious advantage of the salary, it is a precious opening outside the often closed world of the family (and at the same time a way of introducing some fresh air, or at least an outside influence, into the family group). Those who have this chance should not let themselves be talked into an early retirement they have not seriously wanted or planned for: once you are without a job, it is increasingly difficult to find another, so it is important to weigh carefully the risks of a hasty change.

In the absence of a specific problem, there is no reason to question our abilities. If we are qualified and experienced and if our work has been recognized up to now, there is no reason to fear any age-related decline in efficiency and competence. According to a study sponsored by the Gray Panthers, the period of a woman's maximum productivity and efficiency in the workplace is between the ages of forty-five and fifty-five, and following this high point the level falls off only gradually.

It is true that we may sometimes feel that our intellectual functions are deteriorating as we experience memory lapses, mental fatigue, and so on, but we have compensating faculties that play a preponderant role. We may be more skilled than before at making rapid associations, at putting new notions into wider contexts, at developing ideas that are more practicable or imaginative. If our minds are kept active, they continue to function with speed and effectiveness. We also have the accumulated capital of thought processes that have become automatic with long experience, a sure instinct in our choice of methods, a practical sense of organization, an economy and efficiency of gesture, and so on.

Being in form is a question of self-confidence and training: we are to a great extent responsible for the state of our body, mind, and nerves. There is no better way to guard against mental and physical decline than to remain active, and a job outside the home pushes us to do so.

But even if we think we have fully mastered our job, it is essential not to lie back and stick to the routines, following without question and to the letter the methods and intellectual tools acquired over time. Rather, we should constantly update them, adding others better adapted to changing techniques, situations, and individuals. It is useful to challenge certain systems and readjust them to new needs. This is true at all levels of responsibility and for all types of employment.

In 1971, a law was passed in France assuring every employee in the country the right to advance his or her skills and knowledge within the framework of "continuing education." To the surprise of the committees set up to implement the law, there has been a progressive overall decline in interest in the program over the years, despite its advantages and quality. But what is relevant for us here is that it is women, particularly those over forty, who have made the least use of the opportunity, as if they no longer counted on themselves or despaired of progressing.

Age is not a valid excuse; contrary to popular belief, it has little influence on learning ability. Indeed, training is often easier in older age groups in that determination and capacity for work often increase with maturity.

Perhaps these women are tired or so lacking in hope for advancement that they let chances to pursue further training slip by too easily. Or it is possible that, whatever the official policy, women are not encouraged to sign up for the available courses, their employers or supervisors preferring to keep them at their present level of qualification. After all, certain courses or training programs could give them a taste for autonomy, and learning to speak out, first in group situations, may not be to their bosses' liking. It is important for us women to stand up for our rights and seize the available opportunities. We have to remain convinced of our capacity for progress, even if we do not intend to spend the rest of our life on the job.

A number of companies are beginning to organize—above and

beyond purely professional training—courses of "general educa-tion" which are primarily aimed at the employees' personal devel-opment. Why not seize this possibility, if it is offered? Such train-ing enables us to gain some perspective on our knowledge and experience, and encourages us to renew and broaden our ability to confront life's problems.

Technical training and personal-development courses expand our professional competence, support our chances for promotion, safeguard our position, and earn us the respect of our colleagues at the workplace. We have no right to turn our backs on these opportunities.

A word should be said about women in organized labor. At the height of their professional powers, aren't women as well suited as men to exercise responsibility within their union? Women have the advantage of long familiarity with the constraints and prob-lems specific to their trade. If they have been employed in the same company for a long time, they know the networks of communica-tion and internal rivalries, and where the influence lies.

At fifty, we are generally recognized for our competence and stability. We no longer have to take time off from work because of our children. In union activity, all these advantages will make us more credible with the people we deal with. Within these tradi-tional organizations, often frozen in their viewpoints and de-mands, we could bring a new voice and fresh ideas as to the sharing of available work, the management of work hours, work-ing conditions, and many other issues. Personal observation indi-cates that it is the youngest women who take on union responsibili-ties. Why? Why not women of all ages? Why not us, since we are capable?

Many people who have labored long and hard during their work-ing lives dream of retirement. This is the case of countless women who have held tiring, wearing jobs, with long commutes, few attractions, and no possibilities for self-realization. It is hardly sur-prising if they want to claim their rights and benefits as early as possible.

One would imagine that women employees, who between the

home and the workplace are often compelled to put in what amounts to a double workday, would look to their retirement more eagerly than men. Surprisingly enough, this is not the case. Only thirty-seven percent of working women in Europe look forward to their retirement with enthusiasm, compared to forty-one percent of men. After the age of fifty-five, the gap widens, with only thirty-five percent of women as against fifty-one percent of men favorably anticipating retirement.

Could it be that women want to be completely out of the turmoil of menopause and the children's departure from home before having to face a new turning point? Like the parrot who never leaves a rung of his ladder before having grasped the next one with his beak or claw, it is wise to proceed step by step in our readaptations. If we have the choice, we are usually better off not taking early retirement.

A dilemma presents itself when a woman's husband retires (or is made to retire). Should she follow? Will he be able to accept being a "house husband" while his wife continues working and brings home a salary often larger than his retirement pension? Should they put off moving to their retirement home, or should each one live separately?

These questions and many others are being addressed in retirement workshops aimed at helping people foresee their options. It is advisable to start preparing for retirement several years in advance. You need to find out about your rights and the benefits that are due you. If necessary, and if there is still time, certain employment situations must be regularized: some women did not pay attention to the conditions of their contract, and discover themselves to be working as temporaries, independent contractors, or even "off the books."

The husband's retirement, even if expected and desired, can turn out to be a trial for the couple, whether or not the wife is working. We can only imagine what sudden inactivity can sometimes mean for a man, involving a partial loss of identity, anxiety and guilt at seeing his financial resources shrink, and a sudden lack of interests if he did not take pains to develop some when he was still working.

It has been noted that the retirees who remain active and feel good about themselves are those who already had a life beyond the workplace. It does not matter whether it centered on neighborhood activities, the local school, the church, the trade union, sports, or cultural activities. The important thing is that their mind was occupied by something other than the exclusive and permanent concern with their career and their income.

Whatever the case, it is not easy for a man suddenly to lose the principal outlet for his energy and healthy aggressive instincts, to lose contact with the masculine world and find himself in the near-constant company of the ladies' circle. For some men, it is extremely difficult, and their wife's understanding and tact can be the determining factor that helps them get over the hurdle.

The woman must take care not to take over her husband's life. It is all too easy to try to make a child of him, setting him to all sorts of chores or distractions that are not right for him. One must guard against being overly sympathetic or pushing him to get hold of himself at the wrong moment. It wounds him to demand that he remain a champion in bed even while he feels impotent socially or at the other extreme, to avoid his desire when that may be the only reassurance he can find to prove his dignity as a man.

Much discretion and tactful encouragement, much retreat and intervention may be necessary to remain close to him, to find a new equilibrium in this phase of life that is opening. But a constant presence hinders the development toward a new autonomy. The dream of unity—of constant togetherness in all one's activities—is one of the traps of the retirement years. Better to alternate the times of sharing and the moments of privacy in order to maintain the pleasure of being together.

Much of the above also holds true when one of the partners is unemployed. Any expressed or unexpressed superiority on the part of the one who is "holding the fort" is deadly. An excess of kindness or devotion can be equally devastating, only increasing the other's sense of guilt and inadequacy. These are difficult situations, where solidarity is put to the test and the marriage is often made or broken.

Many women respond to the feelings of boredom and uselessness that often accompany menopause by deciding to get a job or go back to work. When we work, we are better protected from ourself, our doubts, our worries, and our family. We feel we are somebody. We have joined the camp of the ones who *act*—the men. For others, a job can suddenly become a necessity because of a death or a divorce that suddenly leaves them with few or no resources.

But if the wish is there for many women of our generation, there are obstacles that make finding a job, and even coming to a firm decision to look for one, difficult. Sometimes there is psychological resistance. If our mother never worked, our ideal image of a mature woman may be that of a wife and grandmother who is always at the disposal of her loved ones. Or we may hesitate to undertake what are considered men's functions, although developing our "masculine" side actually enriches our female personality. Some women can overcome these reservations by identifying with their daughters, who found it normal to prepare themselves for a career and go out to work.

For others, the handicap is a lack of degrees or starting qualifications (how much is a high school diploma or even a bachelor's degree worth without anything else?). This is in fact one of the specific problems of our generation: as adolescents shortly before or during the war, our studies were often haphazard, and those who had to work often started early, under poor conditions; we couldn't wait to quit in order to participate in the baby boom. And until now, when the baby boomers have grown up, this was the focus of our lives.

There are those who have diplomas and qualifications but who stopped working a long time ago. How can they feel "marketable," after so long an interruption, when they know how rapidly and drastically techniques and methods in practically every field have evolved over the past thirty years?

Finally, a good many of those who secretly wish they could go back to work are convinced that age is a formidable barrier, preventing them from even looking for a job. And it is. We mustn't delude ourselves. The obstacles are numerous and considerable. Not all the women over fifty who want a job will be able to find one, and those who succeed will probably do so only with considerable effort.

The age handicap is compounded by factors of social class. Women of modest backgrounds may be able under financial pressure to agree to do babysitting or domestic work, while others simply cannot bring themselves to it. At the other end of the spectrum, upper-class women have a definite advantage in finding work because of a certain air of assurance, not to mention the contacts, that comes with their class.

And for that vast area in between, the middle classes to which almost all of us belong, there is career counseling and job-skills training available through private organizations, community colleges, and the continuing- or adult-education divisions of many universities. Particularly in large urban areas, there may be local government or state programs for older residents including skills assessment, counseling, and help in learning job-seeking skills such as résumé writing, interviewing techniques, and so on. There are also nonprofit agencies providing such services, as well as professional employment agencies.

Some national organizations that will put displaced homemakers in touch with local organizations for job training and counseling include:

THE DISPLACED HOMEMAKERS NETWORK
1010 Vermont Avenue, N.W.
Suite 817
Washington, D.C. 20005
(202) 628–6767

OLDER WOMEN'S LEAGUE
1325 G Street, N.W.
Lower Level
Washington, D.C. 20005
(202) 783–6686

WIDER OPPORTUNITIES FOR WOMEN
1325 G Street, N.W.
Lower Level
Washington, D.C. 20005
(202) 638–3143

NONTRADITIONAL EMPLOYMENT FOR WOMEN
105 East 22 Street
Room 712
New York, N.Y. 10010
(212) 420–0660

If you are really serious, it may be necessary to sign up for refresher courses in your field or to take practical courses teaching job skills.

If you have doubts about how determined or motivated you are to go back to work, or if the possibilities for relearning the profession of your choice seem limited, then it may be wise to invest your hopes and energies and intelligence outside the workplace. But before giving up, perhaps you should have the courage to test your limits and opportunities for yourself, and to seek any kind of active involvement outside the home, paid or otherwise.

• ORGANIZATIONS AND CLUBS •

People join clubs and organizations for many reasons: to make friends, to pursue an interest or passion with like-minded people, to be of service to others, or to promote a cause, political movement, or issues one believes in, such as consumer rights, the environment, women's rights, and so on. The activities can be social, cultural, recreational, civic—all the options are there.

We have seen women who had been depressed, distracted, and vacant become completely transformed within a matter of weeks after joining an organization. They discovered that people still count on them and need them, that their effort and *work* are valued, that what they say and think is taken into account. Suddenly, they feel they are somebody again, and they are happy.

Participation in groups and organizations offers a wide and varied range of possibilities. There are countless organizations in every neighborhood and community, in all fields of interest and activity. You can join as a member, using available facilities and participating in the activities as you see fit, or you can undertake responsibilities within the organization—administrative, planning, whatever is needed. This more active role is often more in keeping with our needs and energies.

If we do take on such responsibilities, donating our time and efforts to serve the goals of an association, we become in effect "volunteers." It is important not to fall into the trap of somehow depreciating this work simply because it is unpaid, donated by a "woman who doesn't work." Unfortunately, volunteer work is sometimes regarded with a certain embarrassment or even shame. In some less urbanized areas or in certain working-class circles, it is still considered a privilege for women "not to work" (what an ironic phrase!). In most places, however, particularly the large cities, there seems to be certain stigma attached to not being "gainfully employed." We encountered the epitome of this kind of guilt in a mother who had raised eight children and who did not have the courage at a women's group session to admit that she spent her time as a volunteer on a crisis hotline, as if this activity were not "serious" enough to mention. Those who have reached the age of wisdom can rail against the new feminist conformity that demands that women have careers, at a time when some young men, though still rare, are beginning in the name of sexual equality to claim the right to remain at home—and presumably also the right to go out for nonprofessional group activities.

Isn't the essential in all of this to have freedom of choice, and then to be able to do what one wants whatever the prevailing fashion? In all these struggles for equal rights, will there always be territory to conquer or reconquer for women to be able to feel liberated and where they want to be?

Certainly, the term "charity work" in the old sense is suspect. It evokes a style of paternalism no longer acceptable today, wherein the socially privileged dispense "charity" to the people, and under the guise of selfless devotion seek confirmation of their social superiority and influence over another social class. It is because of these unpleasant connotations that we prefer the more modern term "volunteer work."

According to a document for internal distribution in France's School for Parents and Educators, "The trend toward volunteerism can contribute to the birth of a new society where men and women at the grass-roots level finally attain the levels of responsibility that are their due. The ordinary individual, until now playing a passive role, takes initiatives, becomes an activist. He becomes autonomous and responsible at the same time. By recognizing his right to the floor, he is given a power, which of itself is to admit the existence of a counter power. . . . The right to believe in something and to invest in it, to find in it one's sense of purpose, is legitimate. Affirming the value of volunteerism can thus appear as a challenge to the existing order, and as such is certainly revolutionary."

The choice of activity one intends to pursue gives very different meanings to volunteerism. It goes without saying that militant or single-issue organizations have a different atmosphere from those engaged in works of charity. To each his or her orientations, with whatever satisfactions they bring.

These satisfactions compensate us to a certain extent for the lack of financial remuneration. The document cited above continues: "Whether or not work is paid does not necessarily enter the picture, since in any case it is 'rewarded' in one way or another. Truly altruistic acts are rare indeed. . . . Solidarity cannot be imagined without mutual pleasure, but we are so imbued with the worship of money that it is difficult for us to admit that there can be other forms of remuneration that are equally valid. Needless to say, this in no way constitutes a justification for refusing to remunerate work that is generally paid."

One of the risks of volunteer or unpaid work is to have it dismissed as a kind of amateurism, however well intentioned. To guard against this and be taken seriously, volunteers must take particular pains to demonstrate their professionalism, imposing on themselves strict rules of punctuality and so on. In working groups of various kinds, every member is important, and those who do not show up disrupt the group's balance by their absence. There is a happy medium between being suffocatingly rigid and overly casual.

It is also essential to acquire the best qualifications possible for the responsibilities we agree to take on. The training of volunteers is increasingly well regarded and professionally conducted, generally by non-profit organizations which are familiar with what is needed and charge lower rates than their commercial counterparts. Moreover, large associations utilizing volunteer personnel also frequently offer specific training to those who join.

Volunteer work is an occasion to develop independence and initiative, to dare to go out and make contacts or carry out needed tasks in the neighborhood or among fellow members.

Some organizations set up groups that meet over a given time period to discuss agreed-upon themes or topics, pragmatic or otherwise, of interest to women in our age group. Such workshops promote a climate of open expression and free exchange wherein each individual, within the context of an unfolding group dynamic, moves toward a more personal response to the questions that trouble her. Through such group sessions and the solidarity they promote, many women who felt alone and helpless are able to regain their equilibrium and find a new sense of purpose and enthusiasm. This new lease on life can lead to a whole range of activities. As a result of one such workshop held in Paris, for instance, one member began working with the blind, another set up a literacy course for immigrants, and three others enrolled in university courses and then organized a women's collective to write a thesis on women in middle age (whose research has proved most useful to us). Others go to museums regularly, do yoga or jog, play bridge or paint. Almost all these women are wives and grandmothers, and their other roles do not suffer as a result of these activities.

One interesting anecdote in this regard: a member of a Parisian women's group became involved in extremely demanding volunteer work when she was about forty-five. Some time later her husband retired and wanted her to leave everything so they could, in her words, "bury themselves" in the countryside. She resisted and then refused. Little by little, her husband developed his own interests and himself became involved in activities that made him drop the idea of moving. He also became less demanding of his wife's time and learned to share the household chores, freeing them both to pursue their respective commitments.

Many women do not favor segregation along age lines, and a number of women's associations sponsor activities and discussion groups aimed at women of all ages, with a consequent enrichment from the mix of generations.

If there are no such associations or groups in your area, or if they do not correspond to your needs or preferences, why not organize one yourself, along with a few friends and neighbors, to share interests, problems, and activities? It can begin in a completely informal way, in someone's living room, and if the idea takes off you can interest the apartment building or street, the neighborhood, the district. At that point you can even contact the municipality, which may find you a meeting place, or you can use the premises of a local church or synagogue. Small support groups or interest groups organized through individual initiative at the grassroots level are becoming more and more common, in contrast to the stultifying giantism of the cities and various bureaucracies. Look around you. Perhaps there already is a pleasant meeting place in your area, a community center of some sort that could be a starting point, an inexpensive place where one can do yoga and various activities can be organized.

Women who become involved in these groups say they have found far more than something to do. They have found a new freedom, a new autonomy and independence of mind, a new way of seeing themselves, a new sense of control over their own lives and destinies.

• GOING BACK TO SCHOOL •

It takes courage to resume college studies after a long interruption, particularly if you do not have a specific idea in mind about how you intend to use your new knowledge or degree. There is no age limit to university entrance, though if you feel rusty it might be wise to test the waters first, immersing yourself only gradually in this great bath of culture and youth by starting out as an auditor. You will be pleasantly surprised at how quickly things come back and at how your accumulated life experience turns out to be an inestimable capital on which to draw. An added benefit of going back to school is that it can bring you closer to your children. For those who want a degree but are unable to become full-time students, many universities have part-time programs where there is no time limit for earning a degree. This is also the case in community colleges.

One interesting experiment is a new center for women's studies at the University of Provence in France. This center offers women who did not finish school and do not work a forum for theoretical reflection and analysis of the problems they are confronting in their everyday lives. The courses bring women, some of whom never had the opportunity to attend college, a wide range of knowledge, since the instructors come from various disciplines—history, economics, law, literature, sociology, or psychology. Information from these fields is taught within the framework of an overall theme chosen for the year ("Women and Knowledge" or "Women and Power," and so on). These themes are fully discussed in class, and the women are happy to be able to bring their personal experience to bear, to be listened to, and to discover or verify that they, too, have something to say, opinions to defend.

This exposure to a university situation gave them the proof that they were still able to learn, to understand a discipline many thought closed to them, reserved for men or for more educated women. In the discussions that followed the presentations, they discovered that they "knew" more than they had realized, but that their knowledge was implicit and disorganized and needed to be made explicit, expanded, and put into a context. It was also reassuring to be able to raise questions in an atmosphere where they had the right *not* to know everything without feeling ridiculous or intimidated. Experiences such as these can arm women with the confidence they need to tackle specialized courses at the university or elsewhere.

• WOMEN AND POLITICS •

Active participation in the workplace, in labor unions, and in clubs and associations can be so many roads leading to an involvement in politics. For the most part, women are not active in political life. Obviously, there are pioneers who have begun to penetrate that bastion of male supremacy, introducing a new tone to the political discourse. But they are still rare and run the risk either of becoming hostages of sorts or of acting as tokens to satisfy the consciences of male politicians.

Without necessarily aiming very high or exhausting oneself with futile ambitions, one can enter politics at the municipal level, which can in fact be a fascinating arena. Except in large cities, it is not that difficult to do. One can play the most effective role for the community at the local level, a role that is also the most immediately satisfying in terms of seeing the results of one's efforts.

CHAPTER 10

Psychological Well-being

HOW CAN WE define so vague a term as psychological well-being? Let us just say that it is the ability to feel comfortable with ourselves and with others, and to feel as consistently as possible energy and enthusiasm for life. Indeed, wanting to live for life itself is a first and essential step to mental health, even if later we need to seek more meaningful reasons for having come into this world.

Those who have not lost their footing up to now, despite the inevitable ups and downs and setbacks of life, will undoubtedly get through this period without too much difficulty, even though at our age we often have to confront a whole series of problems over which we have no control—problems arising from our children, our husbands, our aged parents, the harshness of the times—and which in turn feed into our own stream of fears and anxieties. Other women will have a harder time of it, because their psychological makeup is more vulnerable and they have trouble adjusting to change. But almost no woman is immune to the rather disagreeable awareness accompanying menopause, which is that this biological event has a taste of aging and old age. Everything conspires to bring home this realization, and for some it can be overwhelming.

What strategy can we adopt to confront our aging? What resources can we mobilize to adjust to it and live with it better?

We have already roundly denounced the perverse pressures in our Western societies that despise—and thus implicitly deny—the inevitable aging process. Despite our efforts to distance ourselves from this negative vision of age, we cannot but feel its social consequences and suffer from them. To this must be added an objective reality we have to recognize: to grow old is to see one's life grow shorter, one's "power" threatened. It is to be forced to revise one's ideal self-image or quite simply the familiar image one has of oneself (we have to look at ourselves with glasses on!). All these losses are difficult to accept joyfully, especially since we are not old and these facts are at once accurate and untrue. And the search for a healthy adjustment is not always automatic.

Sooner or later, as we watch ourselves growing older, we are seized by ill-defined and vague sensations we try to push away. But none of us can escape this disagreeable acknowledgment that troubles us more than we care to admit. "I don't want to grow old"—that's the sum and substance of what we are all thinking.

Why try to deny it? Why should we so often have to suppress it? Because of shyness or pride, or for fear of underlining something others may use against us? This denial prevents us from confronting our aging head-on, for what it is, without either exaggerating or minimizing it. And since it exists, we have no choice but to look with a clear mind on what we can do about it.

As human beings, we were made to flee instinctively from our destruction, whether slow and partial or radical, like death. It is normal and healthy for us not to enjoy aging and to resist it physically and psychologically: that is the survival instinct in us. It is normal and legitimate to refuse to travel this road more quickly than our biological destiny requires. But if we do not take a longer view of what is happening to us, we run the risk of missing all the benefits our present age can offer and of neglecting our aptitude for adjustment, which remains considerable.

Adjustment means balancing the withdrawals, the realistic acceptances, and the struggles needed to find a new place for ourself and to come to terms with our present identity. If we have to give up a certain number of things and desires, we can also pick up others along the way. There are gains; there are losses. Do we have to draw up a niggling account, thus prolonging our anxiety?

To make sure that aging does not become an obsession, we have to be on top of, rather than submit to, the present possibilities. We have to exploit them rather than waste them, to evolve and progress rather than flee or stagnate. We have to move ahead to the discovery of a new woman—new, yet at the same time essentially herself.

Every situation of change forces us to renunciations, losses, "mourning." In certain cases, there are no regrets if the estrangement, the completion of a task, or even the death frees our time, our attention, or our heart. Other losses are irreparable, leaving a hole that can never be filled and with which one must live—with which one *can* and *should* live.

No one gets through life without losses. We mature, in every sense of the word, thanks to these ruptures, breaks, and mutations we are forced to cross at every stage, every event, and every period of our lives. If we do not take these into account, we will regress or suffer the consequences later. If we cling to the past or to unreality, we will become a relic, a zombie, or someone who grew old without maturing.

Being realistic in the face of aging is to admit that certain aspects of youth and life are leaving us. The way to mourn these losses is not to suppress the wounds, regrets, or nostalgia, but rather to allow ourselves to feel them fully and to accept them as the price to be paid for looking to the future and moving on. On the other hand, refusal to mourn—acting as if nothing has changed, refusing to recognize that certain things must be abandoned and certain dreams transformed—can only delay the fateful moment of truth and make the ultimate confrontation with reality all the more painful.

We are not advocating a premature old age. But hiding one's head in the sand can be as damaging. It is only by seeing clearly that we can accurately assess the terrain, which battles should be waged and which are futile, what our true possibilities are. A new youth will not magically replace the physical youth that is fleeing us now, but we can fix our desires and hopes on other projects, other enjoyments in other areas.

Sad? Not necessarily. Just different.

At fifty, we are going through a transformation that makes us feel suspended, removed, changed, shaken, uncertain, threatened. But it can also be the occasion for a thorough housecleaning, when we can clear away the crust of conditioning and habits that may no longer be valid. Age in no way prevents us from being flexible and open, and a renewed identity can lie at the end of these mutations.

Have we become what we were meant to be; are we as good as we should have been? Not always. Just because we were successful by a certain standard, growing up to become desirable women, prolific mothers, efficient workers, or admirable wives, does not mean we conformed to our own aspirations or true aptitudes.

Our personality does not necessarily stabilize as we grow older. It can continue to fill out and develop, either through growth of an already well-structured maturity or—after some spadework—through the rediscovery of a freer and stronger identity. If aging means letting go of a certain self-image, a memory of something that was once but is no longer, it equally means breaking free of an illusion that pursues us and does not fit us. This sometimes likable phantom, which was necessary at one time, is our ideal self. It came from our parents, grandparents, traditions, and customs which all combined to endow the child we were with their dreams and inhibitions. This image was necessary for us at one time, provisionally, as a kind of carrot to lure us on. And we struggled in vain so as not to disappoint their expectations. But there comes a day when we are finally capable of discovering the true nature of this wax figure. It is only in breaking it that we can become, finally and serenely, ourself—that is, other than what we seemed until then. Perhaps we are finally free, at fifty—if we have not yet had the strength—to dare to break this ideal image, to separate ourself from this inaccessible and unacceptable old dream.

It is no longer a question of losses or renunciations, but of liberation. True, life can not begin again from scratch—history only goes forward—but women who have been able after this "new birth" of fifty to inaugurate a new social, professional, artistic, or romantic life are not so very rare. In growing beyond the ideal self formed by others, we are by no means depriving ourself of the "ego ideal" so necessary to our mental equilibrium, and which involves our expectations of ourself, the ability to love ourself (and hence be loved), and faith in our possibilities for effort and progress.

In our time, when appearances reign supreme, our slowly fading mask must not be allowed to hide the vitality and the richness of the being inside. We must take care not to fall into the trap of externals. We too must look from within, inventing despite all obstacles the art of being mature and yet alive and vibrant. In so doing, not only do we maintain our physical and psychological well-being, we also change the way others look upon us.

Combating the prejudices of society and the "racist" systems of segregation by age or sex is as much a strategy for growing old with serenity as the more personal struggle to find in ourself a new way of being.

Whether we are trying to maintain our equilibrium and the stability of our moods, or whether we need to recover these qualities that have escaped us, we can increase our chances of success by observing certain rules that are within our reach and that have a direct impact on our mental well-being.

We have spoken at length about health, and we know the costs in physical terms of neglecting our body. But there is also the way we organize our life—a way of either protecting or being hard on ourself. We generally do not know how to use those rare and brief moments we are able to save during the day in order to rest ourself, mind and nerves as well as body. Yet it is essential that we learn how to discharge our tensions without building up that residue of nervousness which, whether or not it is turned inward, can sometimes make of us an electric circuit that is either overloaded or suddenly drained.

Many women with demanding jobs do not manage to find free time for themselves, feeling too guilty to take it from time reserved for their families and unable to do it during working hours. We shall see in the coming pages that the quality of these free moments is more important than the quantity, and that there are certain techniques for using them to better advantage. At home, we are often the victims of our own self-imposed sense of duty, but to carve out some time here can sometimes give those around us a respite too.

Alternating our activities is extremely beneficial to our equilibrium. Yet habit, age, and various other constraints generally conspire to make us repeat the same tasks and gestures used for our work during our periods of relaxation. The professor will use her spare time to read and the seamstress to knit, whereas the reverse would be preferable for each and they both would be better off dancing or playing the flute. The monks of the Middle Ages, for the greater glory of God (and for the greater health and happiness of men), were called upon successively to pray, cultivate the earth, read or write books, and teach, all in the same day.

What would a chart analyzing your daily use of time look like? Have you ever tried to make one? There are several ways of going about it. You can block off your agenda in different colors according to time spent on work, relaxation, cultural activities, household chores, free time, and so on. You can take a few representative days, keeping track for example of a typical week, and divide the budget according to time for oneself, time for others, physical time, intellectual time, spiritual time, and so on.

This little exercise can help us make a more rational use of our time, one more in keeping with our deeper needs. It is the details of our life that can—through the accumulation of constraints or the judicious use of "breathing spaces"—tip the balance toward either well-being or nervous tension.

At our age, we *need* to slow down. If we live in the city or if we work, movement is accelerated for us—sometimes beyond the normal threshold of tolerance. More often than not we are as well adjusted to the pace as can be expected, but today we find the rhythm more tiring than before on our body, nerves, and mind. It is time to change it, if we can. Regardless, we must make ourself do "slowing-down" exercises: in carrying out a task, we can concentrate on the gestures, the task itself, thus distracting ourself from what troubles or enervates us. The activity itself can banish our inner tensions. Getting older sometimes means taking shortcuts.

It is legitimate for us to be even more concerned at this stage of our life about the relationship between our body and psyche. In our search for a better equilibrium, why not give special attention to the various techniques and exercises (or therapy, if need be) that seek to integrate the body and give it the important place it deserves?

We grew up under the lingering shadow of nineteenth-century puritanism, and the attitudes instilled in us about our bodies were usually shame and contempt, or at best "mastery" and "control." Today, the pendulum has swung to the other extreme, and the body has been elevated practically to an object of veneration. It is up to us to find a good balance through any of a variety of methods that aim at achieving harmony and coherence between our profoundly interdependent mind and body.

It is important and useful to take a new look at our body (which does not mean to become fixated on it), paying attention to how it has been marked by our life and character. In following these traces on our body, we can gain a better understanding of ourself and, by relaxing this muscle or eliminating that stiffness, perhaps bring about a certain mental relief. But what separates man from the animal kingdom is the power of speech, and as a human being we may also need to use those abstract symbols called words to break free of our mental constraints and find ourself.

To reconcile these two primordial demands—the physical and the mental—which can be experienced either simultaneously or by turns, we can seek an inner energy and tranquility through various forms of physical or verbal expression. There is no shortage, particularly in large cities, of competent and trained instructors, group leaders, psychiatrists, psychologists, and psychotherapists of every school to help us reach our goal of inner peace. The approaches and methodologies are many, to suit every taste and budget. They can range from dance as an expression of the deeper self to individual or group psychotherapy, from yoga to relaxation techniques, psychoanalytic or otherwise. What all these methods have in common is that they seek to help us recover our unity, our wholeness, through reintegrating body and mind. Among many others, we have selected here a few techniques and ideas that have appealed to many women who are no longer twenty but who nonetheless have no intention of stagnating.

• DANCE •

Dance is one of the simplest, most instinctive means of reaching an inner harmony and should be the most accessible to everyone as an expression of joy, violence, tenderness, and other emotions. This expressive movement of the body is spontaneous in children, but the spontaneity very quickly retreats into a shyness that can be taken for lack of interest. This retreat is doubtless explained by the effect on the child of the mocking or overly indulgent reactions of adults to the very deep, very intimate expression of the self embodied in dance. It is because dance has this evocative power (all primitive peoples use it, respect it, and endow it with sacred qualities) that we can return to it as a privileged means of expression and liberation of the individual.

Let us leave aside the codified dances of parties and balls as well as classical dance, which subjects the body to a strict discipline of movements aimed at perfection. Not that we cannot enjoy them, but their conventions and in most cases their dependence on a partner prevent them from fulfilling the liberating role brought about by free expression such as we are seeking here. Likewise, although we have nothing against pursuing more formal training with a teacher or specialist to improve one's technique and flexibility, our interest here is to use movement to follow our free and spontaneous inspiration.

One of the advantages of dance is the inspiring and stimulating role of music, which takes us away from our surroundings and leads us to our own "journey." It turns the hesitation or even awkwardness of a movement into poetry, and sweeps away the encumbering shyness of self-consciousness and vanity. It can call forth deeply buried emotions, profound and restoring rhythms.

One of the most moving professional experiences one of us ever had was watching the improvised dance of a woman over forty at a group session. No one in the group could have guessed what this sad and beautiful woman had within her, for she remained silent and withdrawn until the group leader asked her about her expectations from the sessions. When she replied, "I can't express it," the group leader, a bit jokingly, said: "Well, then dance it." To the astonishment of the group, which remained transfixed, she spontaneously "danced her life," miming its joys, uncertainties, loves, hopes, and anguishes. There was such beauty, such truth in the vision of this woman who later told us she had not danced like that since she was a little girl.

As in other ceremonies, games, or rituals of primitive origin, dance unquestionably can have therapeutic effects. As one observer described: "I came upon men and women beating drums with powerful rhythms, and I understood the predilection of the Arabs and Berbers for the trance. . . . In the ritual of the trance, there is a therapy that goes far beyond the psychodrama. It is a kind of motor cure through dance, through ecstasy and crying out, through physical release and movement." Without going to that extent, many women probably let themselves go when they are alone and unobserved, and dance, to any kind of music, for themselves, for pleasure and release. They do not feel either abnormal or ridiculous, and indeed they are not—certainly not more so than in trying to recover their abdominal muscles through exercise pushed to extremes.

• YOGA •

Yoga, originating in the East, is more peaceful and individual in its practice, even if it is sometimes taught in groups. It invites us to seek our own physical, mental, and nervous equilibrium through exercises of breathing and relaxation, and through movements and postures which progress gradually in complexity according to the individual's growing ability to perform them. In India, yoga and similar movements have been practiced for millennia to attain philosophical and religious ends. It is of course illusory to believe that we, with our Western mentalities and cultures, would be able, especially beginning so late, to reach the objectives of absolute serenity and disincarnation sought by Eastern yogis. But we can find through yoga easier access to sleep, more unified awareness of ourself, and increased power and control over our body. As a silent and individual technique, yoga may not be right for everyone, and in certain cases it may even encourage the burying of deep problems under an apparent and misleading stillness. It is nonetheless very useful for many, and widely available: most cities have yoga centers, and classes are usually offered at YM/YWCAs and health clubs.

Other schools of physical expression, taking their inspiration from various sources, use music, relaxation, limbering, stretching, and fast movement. The important thing is to have an instructor who is sufficiently trained to assess each person's limits and make sure they are not exceeded. One of the advantages of these various techniques is that, once they have been learned, they can be practiced alone, and just about anywhere.

• PSYCHOTHERAPIES •

None of the above techniques in their usual form can, when used alone, attain the lasting and profound results needed by those who despite medical assistance and strict habits of health have not succeeded in pulling themselves out of deep depression or anxiety. In such cases, more far-reaching therapies are in order.

Other women, without really being depressed, may be finding it hard to control their impulses. Their feelings may be getting out of hand, their anxieties closing in. They can feel restless, adrift, or as if they had some mysterious and throbbing disease.

Finally, there are those who are not prey to this sense of disarray or confusion but who simply find themselves at a turning point in their lives, suddenly curious to have a better understanding of who they are and who they may still become, so as to be able to live freer and better.

Numerous forms of psychotherapy, both individual and group, can respond to these various needs. As already mentioned, psychotherapy is useful not merely to those who are in pain, but also to those who feel relatively good but yet want, with trained help, to delve further into the human questions that concern them.

There are therapies that are exclusively verbal and others that involve the body as well. Although the first practice, which is more traditional, may sometimes be the only one available or may be preferred for one reason or another, we find the second method especially advantageous for women at this particular juncture of their lives.

Is psychoanalysis possible beyond a certain age? Some analysts claim that it is not, and refuse to take on older patients. They say the mental structures, not unlike the arteries, are too rigid by then and that it is dangerous to meddle with them.

It is true that the capacity to tackle analysis and its chances of success depend on the ego's degree of flexibility, but this has little to do with age. There is no reason to assume that our fifty years have deprived us of that minimum of mental agility required for analytic work. There are people of twenty or thirty who could never lower their barriers without risks.

The refusal of some psychoanalysts to accept patients over forty is a reflection of their own problems with age or aging. They should remember that Freud, who already felt old at thirty, did not let that stop him from taking elderly patients. Many analysts report successful results with patients well past fifty.

Some people are not suited for psychoanalysis, and you do not have to be abnormal in any way for it to be risky or a waste of time for you. If you are one of those who believes you can benefit, however, and if your pocketbook permits, you should explore the possibility with a trained and competent analyst.

There are no age limits or restrictions on the other types of one-on-one therapies or group therapies either, provided they are conducted by trained and serious psychoanalysts, psychologists, or group leaders who respect their patients and who have themselves undergone analysis.

On the other hand, one cannot delve into oneself with just any specialist, however competent, and no one would be suitable for everyone, whatever his qualifications. That is why the choice of the therapist or group to whom you will entrust yourself is so important. If you are not well matched, nothing much useful can come out of it. If you are not sure about your choice, meet several different ones before deciding. You have absolutely every right—and you owe it to yourself—to be picky.

Psychotherapy has branched into various ideological currents or schools—practically cults—whose adherents sometimes become rather doctrinaire. They are all more or less, directly or indirectly, descended from Freud through his disciples, orthodox or dissident, and can be followers of Jung, Adler, Schultz, Reich, or Lacan, to name a few. If you are not well informed about these different schools, you won't know which saint to worship! Actually, it is very often the human qualities of the practitioner, beyond his indispensable competence and training, that determine whether the undertaking will be rewarding and beneficial for you.

Never forget that it is *you* who chooses to evolve, to take risks in the hope of attaining greater well-being. The effectiveness of the therapy will ultimately depend on you, and you can always decide to discontinue it if you are not benefitting as you think you should.

• RELAXATION TECHNIQUES •

Methods aimed at consolidating or recovering one's equilibrium include those using relaxation, either as a means or an end. Though Western in inspiration, they seek to obtain part of what yoga offers.

Such techniques teach us to get in touch with each part of our body—our muscles, breathing, and joints—through an "active centering" that aims at bringing about first the awareness and then the relaxation of our entire physical being. The Martenot method grew out of his work teaching music students, who needed to relax physically in order to become completely available to their music.

The Schultz autogenous training technique consists of six exercises to be completed successively during a training that can last anywhere from six to twenty-four months, according to one's aptitude for evolution, one's nervous and psychological type, and the qualities of the "relaxer," who can be a doctor, psychologist, or physiotherapist schooled in this method and if possible attached to an association of research and supervision (of the Balint type).

From these methods, one can gain a relaxation of the muscular tension with which we constantly live, even in our sleep. They offer the experience of feeling pleasure and relaxation by turns, and being able to control them. While doing the exercises, we are filled with wonder at seeing old images spring up from our past, which we are then able to describe and decode. But we will not reach this stage without first making the effort to seek within the depths of ourself the old memories that have formed into psychological knots or blocks obstructing our emotional life and to get rid of them.

Originally inspired by Schultz's autogenous training, a whole school of psychoanalysis has grown up, notably around Michel Sapir in France. The "psychoanalytic relaxation" method it has developed aims at long-range and deep psychoanalytic work without age restrictions.

• NEW THERAPEUTIC TRENDS •

A number of new methods have originated in the United States. Each has its advantages, limitations, and drawbacks.

Bioenergetics, founded by Alexander Lowen, a disciple of the dissident Freudian Wilhelm Reich, holds that the body has a fundamental energy, bioenergy, which manifests itself in the emotions as well as the muscles. Each nervous problem has its physical counterpart. Each chronic muscular tension inhibits an impulse. Feelings are expressed through movement, and each muscle spasm is a barrier that blocks or limits the expression of an emotion.

Similarly, each repressed emotion (anger, desire, et cetera) settles into the body in the form of a blockage which is apparent to the specialist by touch. The therapy thus consists of liberating muscle tension, consequently freeing the aftereffects of the emotional traumas that were at the origin of the blockage.

Bioenergetics uses a number of positions and exercises designed to provoke stress as a first step. These shocks, which can be very trying for the patient, are aimed at attacking the "muscular armor" that has built up over the years.

It does not take much to imagine how developed the armor must be in those over forty, and how strong the jolts and shocks required to penetrate it. If they are violent, as they should be when bioenergetics is strictly observed, one can fear for the physique and psyche of those our age, who get more than their share of stress on any account.

Gestalt Therapy, or the therapy of form and structures, was conceived by Fritz Perls as a form of group (or sometimes individual) therapy. The accent is placed on what happens in the "here and now" and not in the distant past of the individual. Another hallmark of the therapy is the focus on immediate body sensations—dryness in the throat, heartbeat, pressure in the chest, posture, et cetera—as revealing one's most important desires. Gestalt offers the possibility of getting beyond what Reich defined as masochism: "the desire and the fear of bursting." It is thus through focusing the subject on his emotions, on what he feels in the "here and now," that his relation to others, and consequently to himself, is revealed.

The primary goal of the therapy is to lead the subject to become fully aware of what is happening, from second to second, in the contact between himself and his environment, in such a way that he emerges from the confusion or stereotype in which he previously existed and functions according to his true desires, which are now finally identified.

To that end, he must be led to become aware of the mechanisms through which he unconsciously manipulates and blocks creative adjustments to the environment (this is the work on what Gestalt therapy calls resistances). He must be led to extend his present consciousness, his self-awareness, to embrace everything he can experience in the "here and now." This includes his body, and he feels its different parts, what he does, and how he does it. He tries out other ways of behaving. He becomes aware of the outside world through all his senses (sight, hearing, touch, smell). He becomes aware of his emotions and, by that very fact, of what he avoids feeling or confronting. Finally, he becomes aware of how he uses language: as a screen between himself and others, as a substitute for life, or as words connected to his needs and their satisfaction.

Gestalt therapy ultimately leads to responsibility (as opposed to passivity or manipulation). The subject discovers that he can do many things by himself, without depending on others. There are many Gestalt techniques, but three principal types of supports are used:

1. Transactions with others, verbal and nonverbal. Verbal exchanges are encouraged, but only insofar as they refer to what is taking place, or what one is feeling, in the "here and now." Numerous situations are proposed that make it possible to try out types of behavior that are habitually rejected or feared.

2. Dreams and fantasies. The dream is an occasion to discover the gaps in one's personality. Dreams are not only interpreted, but played out in the present.

3. Body work. Meditation enables the subject to recenter himself on what he feels and identify the zones of tension, the parts of his body that are "alive" and those that are blocked. There are also energetic exercises derived from Reichian techniques.

The goal of all these techniques is the ability to speak truly of one's experience, to achieve in one's contact with another a permanent integration between speech, the body, and emotional experience. Gestalt fits into the existential current that opts deliberately for life and freedom. The therapist accompanies his patients on a journey that will lead them to become more alive, freer in their choices, more responsible for what happens to them, more in charge of their lives. He is confident in their ability to function as a whole (body and spirit), as a dynamic process capable of passing quickly from contact to retreat, from activity to passivity, from love to hate.

Gestalt therapy is practiced in both individual and group sessions (ten to twelve people per group) held once a week for about three hours, or in marathon sessions lasting an entire weekend or up to five days. Group sessions provide the occasion to share certain difficulties with other participants who are facing similar problems (difficulties with a spouse or partner, abandonment by a husband for a younger woman, problems with married children or children with unconventional lifestyles, loneliness, physical ailments, and so on). Each Gestalt therapy is unique, since the therapist's task is to follow his patient in his present experience, to be there in order to help him move from confusion to clarity.

In Gestalt therapy, the subject arrives with a certain way of talking and being, with words that finally have a place to be heard and welcomed. At the same time, he brings the density of a body that he will learn how to inhabit all over again. Many come with the feeling that they are unable or do not dare to express themself through their gestures; they feel stiff or blocked in a body they experience almost as an object outside themself, a body quite unlike what they would have wanted. Through group or individual exercises, they learn to let themself go and to enjoy a body more alive to sensations and experiences. For us whose bodies during menopause seem to escape us, to take off in pieces, drained of their substance and energy, this is particularly welcome. The body comes together again, finding a strength hitherto blocked in useless contractions or prohibitions which group work can help identify.

An experience of this kind is also the occasion to learn how one is perceived by others. It is realizing how to go about taking your place or not taking it, expressing your needs or giving priority to the needs of others; in short, it is realizing how you function. It also means having a place where you can try out new behavior, where you can take the risk of doing something different from what you usually do: asking for what you want directly instead of hoping that the other guesses your desires, agreeing to take up the group's time and attention instead of bowing before the needs of others, expressing anger directly instead of accumulating inner tensions or expressing it in other ways. Needless to say, the richness of these experiences depends on the extent to which the participants are prepared to live them, on the changes they are prepared to make. Everyone is responsible for his or her own actions.

If we stress these kinds of activity, it is because we have seen from experience how well they are suited for women our age. Unfortunately, however, they remain the privilege of a limited few.

For most of us, there will be neither crutches nor stimulating aids nor an "awakening" through original experiences. Most women will have to face aging alone, or almost, trying to come to terms with it and bearing up under life's stresses.

A certain detachment or offhandedness concerning oneself will help keep at bay the "totalitarianism" of age. Jean-Marie Domenach, a French writer, notes: "The antidote is faith in the event . . . that is, faith in the possibility that something new will occur. Something whereby I will do something new, thus the opposite of that false newness of advertising and consumerism, which seeks precisely to spare me the entire effort of renewing myself."*

At our age, we have our eyes open. We no longer have to idealize, as if we were adolescents, the perfect body, the perfectly balanced and satisfactory individual, the person who is completely integrated into his surroundings. That doesn't exist, which is probably just as well. But we can call into question some of the unverified "certitudes" that paralyze us, certain habits that eat up our time and energy, exhausting us. Once we have made these economies for ourself, why not use the time and energy thus saved toward fulfilling new desires: the desire to know ourself better, to discover, to deepen our encounter with others, to establish with them an exchange that is simple, direct, warm, and stripped of artifice?

To do so is to give a collective sense to who we are and to our acts, even while accepting our limits and those of others. It is accepting, too, that there are losses, things that do not make sense, failures due not only to our "shortcomings" but to the human condition which made us limited.

*Jean-Marie Domenach, *Ce que je crois* (Paris: Grasset, 1978).

We should always remember that we are ambivalent beings, inhabited by both love and hate, the taste for life and the wish for death. We try to steer our course between these two poles, blinded by fog. But isn't it exciting how with age we learn to know ourselves better and opt with increasing sureness for life?

· CHAPTER 11 ·

Our Relation to Time

THE SECOND PART of this book has focused in particular on the specific steps we can take to better live the years after fifty. Beyond these concrete actions, we can be helped by a certain way of looking at our personal adventure.

Have we reached the "time of sighs"? Or shall we gaily celebrate our fiftieth, this banner year, this seal of age fashioned by time?

And why not? Crossing over into a new decade has always struck the imagination. This time the birthday ritual coincides with a real moment of change. It could push us to feel with greater intensity the progressive erosion of our lives and our human finitude, and open the way for a dreamy nostalgia.

Or the clear awareness of our age can be to our advantage. The time that remains to us is more clearly delineated than it was in the past; we cannot delude ourselves into thinking it stretches before us endlessly, without limits. This realization in itself can provide a key to understanding and utilizing the gift of time. "I don't live in infinity," the philosopher Bachelard remarked in jest, "because one isn't at home in infinity." As for us, we have to take hold of these coming decades in order to inhabit them to the maximum, letting eternity lose itself in the galaxies.

A few questions remain:

How to master time, which sweeps us along in its course, making of it a partner that respects and serves us, rather than an implacable enemy?

How to make each season of our life encompass all the others, without fear or losses?

How to compensate for the inexorable flight of time?

It is not easy to speak of time, even though we are intimately connected to it. In an effort to delimit its relative immateriality, we have to ensnare it in sometimes imprecise words and concepts. We have to use vague images to seize its fleeting contours, even while it takes care to mark us inexorably with a stamp that is all too definite.

For certain philosophers, time is an abstraction; for others, a simple social convention. For physicists and mathematicians it is a scientific fact.

For us ordinary mortals, it is prosaically present through its effects of wear or maturity, through its instruments of measure that either harass our daily lives or do not turn quickly enough to suit our impatience. We are ceaselessly trying to get around the rigor of its imperatives and its laws, and in a certain measure we succeed.

It is the idea we have of time that gives it its true existence in our eyes. Thus, exactly the same information regarding time—the factual "It is noon"—can mean for one of us "Noon *already?*" and for the other "It's *only* noon?" Time will not have had the same reality for both of us. Only the feeling we attach to the duration seems real. The duration underlines comfort or discomfort, interest or boredom, sense or nonsense, stagnation, decline, or progress. Our subjectivity in relation to the time we have lived is what enables us to break its rigidity, to appropriate and give it other dimensions by using it in our way and enjoying it in all its sequences: past, future, and privileged moments.

What reckoning can we make today of our relation with time throughout our own life? In childhood, we often played a game of hide-and-seek against time, where alternately either time was the winner or we were.

At the beginning of our life, the extent of the "playing field" on which our life's course would be run, made up of space and duration combined, seemed to elude our child's eyes, as if we were nearsighted and farsighted at the same time. We were as incapable of evaluating and controlling the present instant as we were of moving about freely, seeing ahead, and orienting our immediate or distant future. Our dependency and our short view gave a strange distortion to temporality. We all remember those immense, virtually undifferentiated segments of time in our childhood, marked only by a few peak events, important or trivial, which punctuated the unchanging seasons with joys, sorrows, and little dramas. Our dimensionless memories were lost in a strange haze. The future—the province of adults—did not reach us except by means of dreams or uncertain promises. We were floating in the expectation of "later, when you're older," even while the reassuring materiality of our family and school taught us to conjugate the present tense in the first person. Our experiences and recollections, which seemed to be quickly erased, were actually accumulating without our knowledge: we could not gauge the silent and lasting part. Such was our initial perception of time.

The first seven years of our life were ones of extraordinarily rapid physical growth: never again will nature impose upon our body a like rate of development and change. It is only in comparison to these years that subsequent evolutions—puberty (albeit far-reaching and rapid) and still more the far slower changes of adulthood and the progressive involution toward true old age—can be judged at their true relativity.

Our development in the emotional and intellectual spheres was proceeding at the same rate. We did not take offense at our "aging" or the loss of our immaturity. The changes, far from being regretted, served to support the experiences that followed.

During adolescence, our ability to appreciate the progression of a human life increased, and time began to take on another consistency. It became possible to project ourself into the future, and consequently we began to feel we had some weight in our individual destiny, although sometimes we needed the occasion of new and often forbidden pleasures to feel this. The moment and its pleasures were lived with deep intensity—but their loss seemed dramatically irremediable.

Some young people today seem dizzied by the vastness of the life that stretches before them. They fear that they will escape war, accident, and disease so as to die in their beds of old age! While awaiting this terrifying prospect, they have difficulty conceiving how they can fill all the empty space in front of them. "Think of your future," admonish the adults, focused on their own plans for the youngster and feeling time running out for themselves. The adolescents of today may thus think they have "too much" future before them and not enough freedom or enthusiasm to use it according to their wishes and projects.

We women of fifty are in exactly the opposite situation. For us, the future is not unlimited. We can realistically assess its boundaries and make serious hypotheses concerning what it can take from us or offer us. We can better tolerate the margin of incertitude or error. The unforeseen is less unforeseeable for us—we confront what happens at least knowing who we are.

We are traveling toward the future with all the baggage of an already long past; it is up to us to dig into it and use what is there. We must take pains to avoid inflicting the weight of our "experience" on those who do not ask for it. On the other hand, if this experience is not for export, it nonetheless constitutes for us an invaluable source of advice, recipes, and warnings which we can consult with confidence. In the light of repeated experiences, we can have an increasingly sure reading of our intuition, that mysterious mental computer which can gather data from the most disparate and imperceptible sources in order to synthesize them, analyze them, and give them back to us in a utilizable and coherent form beyond apparent logic and obvious facts. Why not trust and benefit from it?

Through experience, we may likewise have consciously pinpointed the situations that produce the same effects in us: the psychological traps we fall into, our organic weaknesses, our physical and mental intolerances, or, on the other hand, the partners or places that stimulate us and bring out the best in us.

Through experience, too, we have been able to verify what we could do or be, and to show for it we have a place in the world that contributes to forming a serene image of ourself. It is no small thing to have learned and practiced a profession, to have raised children, to have achieved important or modest works. Whatever happens, what we accomplished leaves its traces and probably lives on, even outside of us.

Past experience is not merely the quantitative sum of a certain number of occurrences and practices which makes it possible to repeat them with more skill and clear-sightedness in the future. Experience is the capacity to predict, to seize, and to feel with an increasingly discerning acuteness the present moment in all its dimensions.

It can be in the intellectual domain, where all the facts one has acquired are more easily organized, selected, and reconstructed in order to be interpreted with increasing accuracy.

It can be in the material domain, where the shortest, most accurate, and most efficient path of movement and gesture is found by the intelligence as well as by the body.

It can be in the emotional or sexual domain, where the awareness of an emotion takes form, where the fear of what will happen afterward is less compelling than the determination not to let the moment lose anything of its brightness. Sensitivity and sensuality develop over time, perfecting themselves in their expression and receptivity, no longer having to waste time discovering or recognizing themselves: they know what they are and what they are not.

It can also be utilizing to the utmost all the skills that have not been ignored, despised, or abandoned on the pretext that we are too old. This can teach us to redirect our energies, transforming the frustrations and renunciations of the past not into bitterness and regrets, but into constructive efforts and expectations to achieve or attempt what we earlier left aside.

Time often brings us a new autonomy in relation to certain family roles and commitments. We fulfilled the most pressing and constraining of our responsibilities toward our children. After our early years as a couple and as a young family, where our identity was often submerged in the family unit and we may have had little interest beyond it, we have reached the stage where a certain differentiation is more in keeping with our aspirations, when we want time for more autonomous, more gratuitous action.

We can carry out the responsibilities that remain to us with greater efficiency and perspective, and perhaps we have learned how to say yes or no or maybe to those who still depend on us. We know now that if we let ourself be eaten up by others' demands on us, we will not be of any use to anyone. It is not a question of postponing or shirking obligations or of trying magically to escape the vicissitudes of life, but of having, with time, acquired the strength and the skill not to allow ourself to be destroyed.

We may come up against the impossibility of realizing a personal goal (is that really a function of age?) but we should not lose sight of the fact that only a portion of the future has eluded us—let us not confuse the whole with the part. A renunciation, even a serious loss, does not mean abandoning everything. If we do not die of it, time will heal us sooner or later (which does not mean that we forget), bringing new possibilities. This is another of the gifts of time: the past has given us experience, patience, and hope. It is by protecting this past as a precious possession that we can make the present grow. But we should not forget either that the future never duplicates the past, and what we learn from the past will never be able either entirely to prevent or bring about the future. The field will always remain open to possibilities, as long as there is life.

The past is also alive with memories, shot through with a kind of magic to which one is sensitive at any age. The freedom of memory is such that it can be sometimes unfaithful, sometimes subjective; the meaning of a past event, whether happy or sad, is always open to reinterpretation. The tricks of the imagination are infinite, and every sorting out or revision is desirable if it helps us to live the present more fully. If there is one precious and inalienable possession we have, it is the free reign of our dreams and fantasies, without regard to age or constraints. We are sheltered from ridicule and prohibitions, and we can wander in time wherever the urge takes us: transcending time is one of the richest and most fascinating functions of the human spirit. But reality is also there to encourage us to live the future.

Time is heavy with promises. What gardener regrets the passage of the days and nights which will make his seeds spring forth from the earth? He is not obsessed by the furrows on his skin, deepened by the sun that gives life to his plants, making the march of time useful and meaningful.

The time that passes marks us with the age it gives us. But do we always realize what point we have reached? "Age takes us by surprise," as Goethe said. This troubling encounter can come suddenly, without necessarily having any relation to a particular decade. It can be weariness weighing on the shoulders of a young mother of twenty-five or the responsibilities a twenty-year-old worker feels when she compares herself to her carefree contemporaries. Which of us has not felt old at times before thirty? These experiences, generally fleeting, vanish with a change of mood, situation, health, or partner, and we resume life with the age we feel, our chronological age forgotten.

Then suddenly we are hit by *reality*—the age there is no mistaking and which, to boot, we have been made to understand is the "bad age." The effect will be all the more painful if we have not had the time or courage to see it coming and to look it squarely in the face. We risk no longer coinciding with the illusory or abstracted image of ourself we had become comfortable with.

If for some women the failure to recognize the fateful accumulation of years is deliberate, a willful act of self-delusion, for most it is due instead to a kind of self-effacement, a focus on things other than themselves. What were they doing with their time so as to lose sight of its discreet but relentless progress within them and outside them? How did they allow themselves to be caught by surprise, to wake up one morning and find themselves fifty, in the grip of new and disturbing physical sensations?

Most women, by the very nature of their lives, scatter their time, distributing it here and there without being able to save enough for themselves. They spend it on their partners, toward the well-being and continuation of the couple, the growth and healthy development of their children from cradle to self-sufficiency. So much time, so much life was invested without their even realizing it—they simply took it for granted. For many women, professional responsibilities were added to these others, and between their jobs and their homes they had no free time at all. Not that they did not find a great many satisfactions, but there was none of the free utilization of time one needs to make plans, to organize one's life and one's future. So it was that all these tasks and ties were able to mask the inexorable arrival of time.

But once the age is there, with our fifty springtimes and the others that will be added so quickly, how are we going to react? When confronted with age, we are neither free nor equal.

Some women take it lightly. For them, "evil to him who evil thinks"—it's as good an age as any, with its own harvests and fruits. These serene and optimistic women often began life with few advantages, either physical or social or even intellectual, and were able to make something of themselves by their own efforts. They feel little regret for a youth that held fewer joys than their maturity. For them, middle age is an occasion to reckon up successes that surpassed all expectations. What difference does age make, so long as they have their health and ability to work?

Others saw themselves as so heavily weighted down with work, children, and anxieties that they thought they would never be able to recover later. To their great surprise, not only did they hold their own, they also forged a personality and sense of worth, and even became more attractive.

At another extreme are the women who were always pretty or beautiful and whose self-image is bound up in their physical appearance. Their situation is even more difficult if they work in areas that glorify and exploit youth and beauty, thus making their jobs more precarious with the physical deterioration brought on by aging. This is often true of those working in fashion, hairstylists, hostesses, models, certain types of saleswomen, and actresses (except those who change to new kinds of roles to suit their age, and whose personality affirms itself with time).

For most of us, who are neither beautiful nor ugly, brilliant nor stupid, and who age by sure, small steps, it would be useless to feign indifference or to convince ourself we are resigned. There are days we find it painful to look at ourselves in the mirror, others when we think we don't look so bad or even pretty good. We vacillate between melancholy and serenity depending on the days and the hours, people and things, what seems to be happening on the surface and what is happening inside our bodies and heads. Our dearest wish and effort is to be able to prove—to ourselves as well—that today we can still be loving and loved, useful and alive. If we find any encouragement, we will do everything in our power to make sure that our age remains, in its fashion, a graceful age.

We know, since we are realistic and not without humor, that certain days we will be "old biddies" to the young trendsetters and "grannies" without interest to the more oblivious of our male contemporaries still setting their sights on other age groups. But we also know that our husbands, lovers, and friends will continue to see us with tenderness and conviction as "my sweet" or "my beauty"—and for a long time yet. Love is blind, they say, and why not believe it? Let us not put off those who still find us to their liking, those who attach less importance to the truth of our wrinkles than to the truth of the feelings we inspire.

We are perfectly free from time to time to use some artifice, if it amuses or reassures us or pleases a partner as a sign of catering to his desire. We should not give these whims either too much or too little importance, and we should certainly not be taken in by them. We are at an age where excesses in style and makeup do not sit well. Ridicule is far more deadly for the old than for the young, and it is not thus that we can recover past successes.

A woman's age and menopause are frequently blamed for a marital breakup or crisis among our contemporaries, but they are a flimsy excuse, a transparent alibi for the explosion of a conflict that has often been brewing for many years. The couple needs a scapegoat so as not to have to call into question the entire system of their relationship, and the woman's age and aging serve the function.

Time has given us so much: seeing our children become adults; the house that, through our labor, was built or did not collapse; the love affairs and the friendships that were not worn but strengthened by the years. We have tastes, styles, culture that have come to bear our own stamp. Which of us does not feel more substantial, more solid, at least more clear-sighted than we were at twenty? Then why would we want to repudiate our age? Far more important than showing off or impressing others with small deceptions is to be at ease with what we have become year after year.

What does "to be of one's time" mean? We sometimes confuse it with staying young or being able to communicate with the younger generations. It thus becomes a question of conforming to the fashions, values, and behavior—in short, to the mass culture—of the present.

Are we going to deny, at our age, the earlier segments of our life, with their experiences and what at the time marked us, captivated us, or helped us grow? Should we now identify with the current movements to the point of denying our own nature and culture? Why should we not feel sufficiently sure of ourself to be able to select in each successive wave what seems to fit us best, what we can embrace the most sincerely and the most freely? One can be "up to date" through conformity and cowardice, a passive chameleon to all the trends of the hour, no matter how absurd or scandalous. We should know that we have reached an age where our best advantage is to be what we were meant to be, to have built our own and original personality while remaining completely true to ourself.

If the fifty-year mark is frightening and upsetting, the generations ahead of us report that for the most part the coming years will be easier and more peaceful. Simone de Beauvoir, who was dramatically preoccupied with aging in her writings around fifty, later confided: "The first thing that strikes me, if I consider the ten years that have passed since I completed *Force of Circumstance,* is that I don't have the impression of having aged." The prospect of an easier time ahead can help us along, but the important thing is not to waste or lose this crucial segment of our life.

The "age difference" between individuals of different generations living and working side by side has been a fact of life since
time immemorial, and has been not only generally well tolerated
but even institutionalized through the development of roles each
member is called upon to fill.

But today there seems to be a consensus on "easing out" the
oldest. It is as if adults over forty are being struck earlier and earlier
with obsolescence in all fields and should stand aside for the coming generations.

A gulf is thus deepening between adult generations, mutually
isolating them from one another, the older ones excluded earlier
and earlier from the work force (through early retirement plans)
as well as from romantic possibilities (considered indecent or pre-
posterous at their age). This unnatural division could become
more destructive than the famous—though somewhat fictitious—
"generation gap" between adolescents and adults. Adolescents
remain so dependent on adults, whether they admit it to themselves or not, that this in itself constitutes a contact, a connection.

We should not believe that men and women shunted from the
active centers of life are going to sit back and do nothing about it.
They constitute a force capable of organizing itself into a counter
power in political parties, associations, clubs, pressure groups, and
so on. They can have an electoral weight that will enable them to
make unexpected choices in favor of those who defend their place
in society. It is important for men and women our age to stand by
them in their tribulations, which are an unjust consequence of
their age. We do not want ourselves to be excluded from the
future.

The difficulties connected with age differences can also be felt
within the context of the married couple. Sometimes it is a question of an actual age difference, which become more visible with
the passage of time. But it can also be a problem between partners who are contemporaries, but who are not aging at the same
rate.

In the past, men were absolutely confident of their sexual superiority over women and consequently remained active longer. It is
true that male fertility, which men too often confuse with sexual

ardor, can theoretically continue into the most advanced age. This assumes, however, an absence of self-doubt, which once implanted can result in a total withdrawal from sexuality, particularly if it follows upon other episodes of impotence.

It appears that the situation today is reversed: chances are that women will remain in better spirits and in better shape sexually than men the same age. At fifty, many of us have achieved a certain material freedom with the departure of the children. In addition, we often enjoy a psychological independence born of our maturity and enhanced by the battles waged over the last decades by women for women.

Women of our generation, generally rather repressed during adolescence, were frequently "late bloomers" sexually and initiated into sex by older partners. Many hope to make up for this slow start and are not prepared to renounce the desires that age has not managed to extinguish.

Aging and the long years of married life may not affect the two partners in the same way, and an age gap can accentuate the difference. One partner may lose interest or seek satisfaction elsewhere; the other, still looking to the mate for shared pleasures, may hope to arouse him (or her) to participate.

Men are often physically more fragile than women, despite our problems of menopause. They do not always follow as willingly in our enthusiasms and our desires for outings, get-togethers, or sporting or cultural activities. They are tired, perhaps disillusioned. If we wear them down with our impatience and insensitivity, we may regret it.

We have no desire to gloat over our advantage, because it is *with* our partners (and no longer *through* them) that we would like to live and share some of our interests. If they are so touchy concerning their male image, it is because their upbringing allowed them scarcely any weakness or margin of error. Since adolescence, women expected them to be stronger, more cultivated, more intelligent. In their own eyes, the slightest weakness meant losing face and the respect of the other sex. Today, we should be aware of the burden that was placed on their shoulders. We should love them enough to help them accept themselves as they are, that is, more vulnerable and limited than they would like to be, but perhaps more understanding of the weaknesses of others.

We must hope that they will still be strong enough to tolerate our power, our endurance, and our desires. If we care for them, we must try to clear up any misunderstandings concerning our respective expectations and possibilities, and try to talk out where we are different and where we complement one another. Otherwise, we will lose each other, perhaps seeking through younger partners what we still would have been able to give each other, if we had tried.

Beyond the couple, what is happening around us, particularly in our ties to the next generation? Do we recognize it as the one we have produced?

If young adults sometimes seem strange and alien to us, the split between them and us is very often due to our own intolerance: how do we react to their new ideas, their casual attitudes regarding work, "fidelity," childrearing, and what we call "values"? What do we think of their offhandedness?

Can we not appreciate the fact that young women today are able to demand from the very outset that share of autonomy we are only now discovering for ourselves? In particular, they have altered the distance between themselves and their children (our grandchildren): they are closer in the sense of free exchange—speaking out, arguing, expressing their feelings more easily than in our day—but more distant in that they dare to entrust the children to day-care centers or nursery schools without guilt. The children do not seem any the worse for their mother working and their father doing the dishes (sometimes!) or getting them ready for school. There has been no evidence to date that these new habits are harmful to the children.

The new ways of bringing up children (which are not, as is often believed, particularly lax) confer other benefits as well: the young parents know how to say no and do not let the children run their lives. There is less prudery and sexual repression today, and the loosening of the rigid hierarchy between parents and children, which did not guarantee mutual respect, is certainly an improvement. Class and race prejudices have diminished, with children now being allowed to have playmates of all social backgrounds and family situations (in our day, relations with the children of single or even divorced parents were frowned upon).

If our daughters have been able to evolve toward these new ways of being a woman, perhaps it is because we ourselves carried within us, even unknowingly, a foretaste, a desire for renewal in our destiny as women. Our children did not fall out of the blue; we had our role in pushing toward this evolution. Let us not now deny its fruits.

We should not forget that the age of fifty seems frightening to younger generations, who begin to fear growing old from the time they reach thirty. It is to us that they will look as witnesses and examples of the value of each stage. (We were surprised, in preparing this book, to find that women much younger than ourselves were interested in our work.)

The difficulty of balancing time for work and time for rest, busy moments and quiet moments, and of alternating them in a use of time that suits our real needs is a phenomenon of modern life that becomes particularly relevant for us when we are around fifty.

Are we really taken in by our astonishment when we say, with a nostalgic sigh: "How quickly time flies!"? Yes, it does pass, imperturbably, and we cannot stop the hourglass, whatever our stratagems. On the other hand, we do sometimes seem to have the talent to ruin the time we are given.

Are we locked into this frenetic haste—not only the haste imposed on us by circumstances, but that which we bring on ourselves through our disorganization or inability to resist distractions? We often suffer anxiety at finding ourselves more or less trapped in doing a slapdash job, which results in guilt and suffocation. We know that everything loses its urgency with time. Yet we unresistingly throw ourselves into this fever, this compulsive binging of activity and consumption that was developed and then encouraged by our entire society. We can be caught up in this mad race either directly through our jobs, or through our husbands, whose absence, impatience, or unavailability we have to put up with at home.

Today we are pushing the system to its outer limits, with a wear and tear on our nerves and body that is getting out of hand. And the day we retire or become unemployed, on what are we going to unleash this tightly coiled spring of unhealthy energy and haste?

A great many of us need to revise—indeed to reinvent—the balance between our private and professional lives, even at the expense of resisting the tyranny of certain jobs or employers. We are a long way from the supposed "allergy to work" of the new generations. Beyond our absolute obligations, we should increasingly try to distance ourselves from others' expectations of what we should be. School, professional life, and family responsibilities gave us little scope to invent our lives—the paths were mapped out in advance, and imaginative departures were scarcely tolerated. It is now up to us to discover, if we have not already done so, the activities and interests that best correspond to our desires and abilities, and to fight if necessary to make them respected.

There is another reason behind this time-devouring frenzy: the need to prove our importance and usefulness to others as well as to ourselves. Are we one of those who have to consult a social calendar, already filled weeks in advance? What are we trying to prove? What are we running away from? Ourself, our worries, boredom? Perpetual motion does not help any of these.

We recognize that women who are always in a rush, always "busy," were brought up with a strict taboo against "wasting time": in school, at home, at work, even on vacations. Dawdling, "fooling around," and daydreaming were all somehow guilty occupations, since these little freedoms escaped the control of others.

However we ourselves feel about our constant haste, are we aware of the painful effect it produces on those who are less occupied? It constantly confronts them with the image of the permanent saturation of our time, making them feel "out of it," all the more useless and in the way. They would not dare ask us to spare a moment of this time, so precious because so rarely obtained.

Young people complain bitterly about how unavailable adults are in terms of time and ability to listen. They do not find our activities so important or so interesting that they should be sacrificed to them. Old people, too, are waiting, with sadness and resignation, for a little time for them.

And for ourselves, adults in the prime of life, are we aware of the mental and physical tension, to say nothing of the fatigue, brought about by this permanent haste? How much of our insomnia, headaches, or indigestion is caused by this poor management of our time? Life under pressure leads to aggressivity, sometimes to depression, and in any case to the chronic ill-humor characteristic of too many women our age. Are we sufficiently aware of this alienation?

Can we learn how to slow down, to vary our pace, to provide gaps in our use of time or busy time that is meaningful, respecting our tastes, our need for variation, and our biological rhythms? We can plan for moments of serenity and make them happen. Women generally have a sufficiently developed sense of duty to do what is necessary, without adding that extra something that not only exhausts them but leaves those around them exhausted and saturated by their dedication.

The French scientist Joel de Rosnay explains, "We have to relearn how to waste time in order to know better how to economize it collectively. In our civilization of hurry and waste, the contemplation of a landscape, a conversation with a child, the practice of a sport, or simply thinking seems a waste of time. But how many fruitful ideas, how many creative reflections and new hypotheses were born of just such moments? . . . Individual creative action is what makes it possible to compensate the loss of time, for every original work is analogous to a reserve of time."

Our fiftieth year is the ideal time to take stock of the future. It is also the ideal time to work at things that can determine its course. The first is preserving our capital of health. We know what areas need attention and where we must be careful. Next comes knowing our limits and capabilities. We must become aware of and develop gifts that were neglected or unknown until now.

It is the time to choose our true measure, to consent to our aging and at the same time to struggle against it, without being destroyed by it. It is time to rethink and readjust our philosophical and political positions, avoiding both a paralyzing skepticism and the repetition of inappropriate past choices. There is no plan for the future without a sense of utopia.

This is also the age to think about our death: thinking about it won't make us die, and in any case death is written into our genes. A global vision of our life is now possible, for the past delineates the future and we can better see the coherent unfolding of our existence. It is thus that we can seek to orient our death toward a human and dignified end: we can make clear our wishes and convictions to those around us while we are in full possession of our faculties. This realistic view of our ultimate destiny is by no means at odds with an invitation to live life to the fullest. We are far more able now than we were during our childhood or youth to appreciate the value of a serene and happy moment.

If we feel worried or threatened by our tomorrows, let us try to learn the wisdom of the biblical saying "sufficient unto the day is the evil thereof," or, more simply, "one day at a time." There are always times of waiting when we can no longer influence the course of events, so we must let it go, let things happen. This is not giving up, but a way of freeing ourself from a sense of powerlessness and anxiety, and learning to take what the present offers in terms of respite, peace, or pleasure. At our age, why ruin the moments of well-being or pleasure that come our way? We know their fragile and ephemeral nature, and we know better how to recognize them. Such moments are already there, very simple, very immediate. It is the moment when we slip into our bed, freed from our clothes and our chores after a tiring day. It is the moment when our body returns to us, the moment of relaxation, the moment of first contact with the cool sheets or the warm body of a partner, the moment we decide whether we want to read or sleep. It can also be the moment when the body drifts off into weightlessness. We can glide there, ageless, timeless, with free thoughts and fantasies sailing through space. We succumb to the pleasure of the moments of suspension between wakefulness and sleep, as we slip softly into oblivion.

There are the pleasures of orgasm, of a hot bath, of the sunlight that flickers an instant on the skin or is reflected in the eyes. The simple pleasures of a well-prepared meal, the brush of a child's lips or the feel of his skin. The pleasure of working the soil, of planting, harvesting, puttering around the garden. The flush of happiness at an unexpected idea, a piece of artwork, a person, an event. To find oneself creating something, and enjoying it. And all the many other things that we experience.

All that may not add up to happiness. We do not all have the ability to find happiness to the same degree and for the same reasons. But it is good, for ourselves and for others, to know how to seize wherever we can the simple sensation—whether subtle or intense—of being alive.

The art of living can be one of the privileges of our age. Despite the harsh realities of the present and the uncertainty of the future, let us cultivate and cherish as our most precious possessions our freedom and our taste for life.

Let us, as women constantly evolving, learn better than we have in the past to appropriate for ourselves our future.

Index